# MEETING GOD

*Elements of Hindu Devotion*

# MEETING GOD

*Elements of Hindu Devotion*

Text and photographs by Stephen P. Huyler

Foreword by Thomas Moore

*Yale University Press    New Haven and London*

Design: Joseph Guglietti Design, Santa Fe

The serif texts are set in Janson, the sans-serif texts
are set in Meta, and the book was composed on an
Apple Macintosh by Joseph Guglietti and Lehze Flax.

Project Management: Joseph Publishing Services

Printed in Italy by Conti Tipocolor


Library of Congress
Cataloging-in-Publication Data

Huyler, Stephen P., 1951–
Meeting God: elements of Hindu devotion /
Stephen P. Huyler;
foreword by Thomas Moore.
    p.   cm.
Includes bibliographical references and index.
ISBN 0-300-07983-4 (cloth: alk. paper)
ISBN 0-300-07984-2 (pbk: alk. paper)
1. Hinduism—Rituals. 2. Worship (Hinduism).
3. Gods, Hindu.
I. Title
BL1226.2.H89   1999
294.5'43 — DC21                    99-11035
                                        CIP

A catalogue record for this book is available from the
British Library.


*The paper in this book meets the guidelines for permanence
and durability of the Committee on Production Guidelines
for Book Longevity of the Council on Library Resources.*


10 9 8 7 6 5 4 3 2 1

OPPOSITE
HUBLI, DHARWAR DISTRICT,
KARNATAKA

Ganesha, Remover of Obstacles and
Lord of Beginnings.

PAGES 2/3
VARANASI, UTTAR PRADESH

Predawn prayers on the banks of the
Ganges River.

PAGE 4
PADMAPODA PURI DISTRICT, ORISSA

Invocation ceremony for the Goddess
Chandi.

PAGE 11
SRIRANGAPATNA, MYSORE
DISTRICT, KARNATAKA

The final *puja* to the God Ganesha
before his image is immersed in
the river.

PAGES 14/15
SINGASPURA, KURDHA DISTRICT,
ORISSA

Schoolchildren celebrating the *puja*
of Saraswati, Goddess of Learning.

PAGE 16
NADAKKAVAL ALAPPUZHA
DISTRICT, KERALA

Lamps lighted to welcome the arrival
of the Goddess Bhadra Devi.

*Truth is one; the wise call it by many names.*

—Rg. Veda 1.64.46 (trans. Diana Eck)

*I dedicate this book to the true loves of my life: my wife and soulmate, Helene, and Bharat Mata (Mother India)*

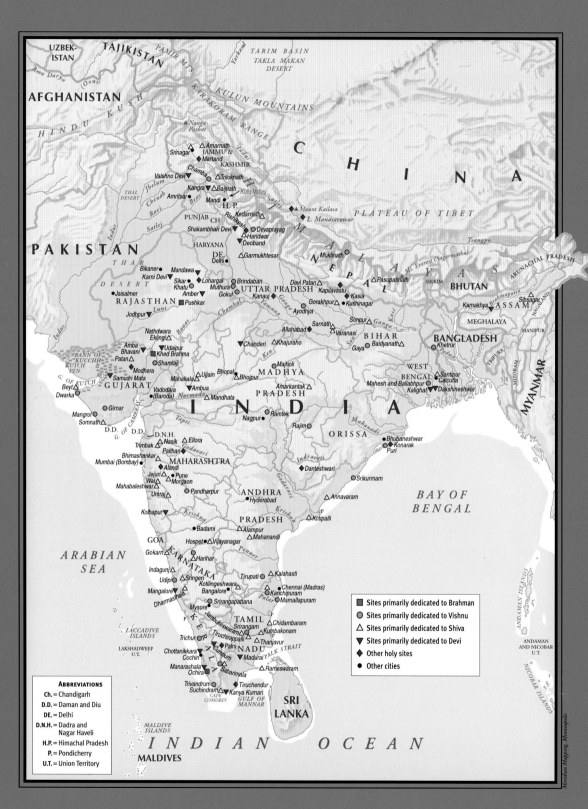

# HINDU SACRED SITES

# Contents

In our day it is difficult to reconcile the idea of meeting God, encountering the Divine in a real and tangible way, with the current mythology of modernism, which winnows out a religious way of living and thinking as superstitious, anachronistic, or naive. Because we sift out the sacred as we build a culture and shape our lives, the religious impulse grows dry and hard in the established churches and becomes suspiciously spellbinding in new spiritual cults and practices. We seem divided down the middle: a world of empirical studies and technological wizardry on one side, a realm of broken and forgotten images, if not sheer vacancy, on the other.

Our trust in technology and empirical methods, along with the resulting focus on literal fact, is indeed our myth. People have always lived their mythology as though it were simple, literal truth. To be reflective about the deep stories, images, and memories that form us is to lose something of the intensity of belief. Science has its doctrines, its priesthood, and its rituals, but the object of its worship is not open-ended. Whereas religion usually looks for an opening to the eternal and infinite, science hopes for closure and places its faith in the capacity of the mind to sew things up. It prefers finity over infinity. The result is a world where the ego is at home and consciousness a supreme goal.

Today the various spheres of daily existence still have their glow and glamour, a word that once meant "magical spell." Things still drive us crazy with desire as we shop in enchanting malls and drive in microcosms called automobiles—self-movers. In many ways our cars seem to be extensions of our egos. Sports take us out of flaccid reality and into the undeniable charm of game and fantasy. Television and movies offer us stories that waken the eternal themes found in religion, but here these motifs are heavily disguised, so that we respond to them as entertainment but don't quite catch the deep spell of religion.

The magical world of India that Stephen Huyler evokes with his wondrous photography and devotee's manner of observation shows us that it is still possible to live in the world religiously. Some religions accent the intellectual or the emotional, but the Hinduism we see and feel in this book is the work of the body and the imagination, both held as sacred and both powerful avenues to the Divine.

I have been familiar with Stephen's work for some time now. I came to it after many years of reading Hindu scriptures and enjoying the mystifying stories of the Gods and Goddesses. In this presentation of Hinduism I deeply appreciate the coming together of two potent spheres: the hard work of daily survival and the limitless imagination that gives such vitality to ritual, story, painting, shrines, statuary, temples, and gestures, to note just a few elements of *puja*. Here religion is colorful and entrancing. It is practiced by ordinary people on ordinary days and usually in ordinary places, but all that ordinariness is transformed by an imagination for the infinite that is vivid, passionate, and remarkably sophisticated, and articulated with great subtlety.

It may be tempting to regard this valuable book as a coffee table tour of Hindu India, to place it in the discovery channel of the mind. That would be a mistake. Just as Stephen confesses that he formerly kept a distance, which he justified as scholarly objectivity, as he observed puja over the years, so we the readers might persuade ourselves not to see the real spirituality in these photographs and descriptions. We might defend ourselves against the challenge of finding real religion in these pages or indeed an invitation to reconsider our own secularism.

Apparently the people of India have no need to keep their religious sensibility to themselves. Unlike some anxious believers around the world, they have been able to avoid the paranoia that often accompanies religion. On our part, we could open-mindedly consider the challenge to secularistic modernism offered so beautifully in these pages. I am not suggesting conversion to Hinduism. Far from it, I am speaking about my own reaction to this work: the sense that my life could be richer, more tuned to the eternal through simple ritual and poignant images, through a more radical refusal of the modernist paradigm and a deeper trust in my own religious imagination.

As a former psychotherapist, I am painfully aware of the many struggles that modern men, women, and children go through just to make it through life. Drugs, divorces, violence, suicide, aimlessness, drudgery, endless moving, food problems, illness, crime, prejudice, and injustice—these are signs of the times, and yet rarely if ever do we consider that they may all be due to the loss of an intelligent, grounded religious way of life. I am not talking about beliefs and allegiances and certainly not about anxious and defensive claims to truth and salvation. We still worship idols, though they go by other names.

It is my conviction that our personal and social problems can be solved only in the context of religion, because these issues are all so deep that they transcend psychological and technological solutions. We need nothing less than a renewal of religious imagination, and to that end there is much to be learned from the concrete, touching, simple Hinduism filtered through the brilliant lens of Stephen Huyler.

So I would recommend not perusing this book lightly or studying it with academic distance. The material here, though unfamiliar to most readers, is all about our own heart and soul. We could reimagine our daily lives, our goals and hopes, the ways we educate our children, and simply the way we spend our precious time all in the light of the remarkable images and touching attitudes of the people pictured here.

After meditating on the images contained in this volume, I feel a certain envy for people who can live so gracefully in the combined realm of spirit and ordinary reality. It wouldn't take much for me to become this sort of Hindu, and I'm certain that in the process I would also become much more deeply Christian. The Hindu doesn't merely tolerate other religions—that is a modernist way of thinking—but much more substantively, the Hindu recognizes that the intimate mutuality of religions intensifies one's own inherited or chosen practice.

I would like to ask the reader: What is your puja now? What could it be? Select one photograph in this book and find out how your devotion to your soul, your family, your community, and your world—to life itself—could be articulated and given form. Don't allow yourself ever to be too far from holy fire, sacred water, and images of the Divine. Make this puja your own, and in your own small way waken the soul in your world through small, mindful methods.

*Thomas Moore*

I had been to Padmapoda, a village in eastern India, a number of times previously to visit the family of a close friend. Each time, I had been taken to see the sacred tree that embodies the local Goddess, Gelubai, the deity of the community. This new experience was an unprecedented honor: being allowed to witness the ceremony of invocation in which the dynamic power of the supreme Goddess Chandi was requested to subsume and transform that of the local deity. It was a very special ritual, enacted on rare occasions to implore the aid of the Goddess in overcoming a difficult domestic problem. My friend Babu Mohapatra, understanding my wish for insights into Hinduism as preparation for writing this book, had arranged this special *puja*. The entire ritual had already taken two priests two hours: preparing and dressing the image of the Goddess, drawing a sacred diagram upon the ground and building a fire on it, and feeding that fire with clarified butter (*ghee*), all the while singing her names and praises. As a middle-aged cultural anthropologist and art historian who had already spent more than half my life studying India, I prided myself on my objectivity. I might feel empathy toward a particular subject or situation, but as a scholar I tried to distance myself to observe and take note.

Despite my resistance at that moment, as the fire flared brightly and the spirit of the Goddess was invoked to enter the tree and be available to the village, I actually felt her presence. I felt a change in the atmosphere: a palpable sense of power vibrating throughout the area surrounding the sacred tree. It was a type of pulsating energy, the strength of which I had never before sensed in my life. I was completely surprised, overwhelmed beyond any expectation. In that one moment I, who had come as an observer, had become a participant. That insight altered and enriched my perception, allowing me to release decades of self-identity as an objective outsider. By being fully present and receptive to an experience so different from anything that I had been raised to understand, my personal and professional life was changed. I was transformed.

My life has been filled with abundance. I arrived in India on my twentieth birthday to spend the next seven months living in homes throughout the Indian subcontinent. It was a seminal experience that provided the basis for my next twenty-eight years of field research. I have always found the Indian people to be remarkably hospitable, opening their hearts and their lives to me with generous candor. By profession I have conducted a cross-cultural survey of the material culture of rural India for years, crisscrossing the country in pursuit of the comprehension and documentation of Indian folk arts and crafts. People have always invited me into their homes, to witness and share in their private lives and feelings. From the beginning I have been in awe of the innumerable household rituals I have been privileged to observe. I have been fascinated by Hindu spirituality, by the ways in which conscious awareness of the Divine permeates every aspect of daily and seasonal life. But for a young American raised in a strong Christian family, much of it seemed obtuse and confusing.

My research and photography of Indian creativity enabled me to focus on the material world, to learn to understand Indian culture through the objects it produced. But as all crafts in India are believed to have a spiritual content and purpose, my awareness and understanding of Hinduism grew as my work evolved. Two of my previous books have dealt with sacred arts. *Meeting God* had its direct genesis in an exhibition I proposed and co-curated at the Smithsonian's Arthur M. Sackler Gallery entitled "Puja: Expressions of Hindu Devotion." Sacred Hindu objects, drawn largely from the private collection of Paul Walter, are displayed as they were originally meant to be seen: not primarily as works of art (although many are indeed beautiful pieces) but dressed, adorned, and installed in shrines. The exhibition, which opened in 1996 and is still on display, attempts to inform visitors of many of the previously misunderstood aspects of this major religion. The gathering of materials and writing of the text for the show (descriptive panels and labels) was the most difficult task I have ever undertaken. It required a simple and yet enticing synthesis of what is perhaps the most complicated and misunderstood group of religions in the world (collectively called Hinduism). The experience of working on that permanent exhibition inspired the traveling exhibition and this book.

I have spent the past five years gathering material in India for these three purposes. During this period my life has been deeply enriched. From that first experience of participating in the worship of the Goddess Chandi in the sacred tree in Orissa, my perceptiveness has grown immeasurably. Now when I am invited to attend a sacred ceremony, I no longer withhold myself in critical appraisal. I am fully present with all of my senses to absorb the ritual, to feel the full experience. I realize now that my earlier distance was merely the consequence of my own limitations. The many Indians with whom I have interacted have always invited my full participation. For years I held myself apart. My Western heritage and my unconscious miscomprehension of image worship blinded me from deeper understanding. Today I believe that I can still retain a grounding in and deep respect for my American Christian background while being receptive to the many facets of Hindu spirituality. I can admire and even be in awe of the ways in which the sacred permeates the lives of the Hindu people while still maintaining strong attachments to my own home, family, friends, culture, and ideals. Awareness of one only enriches awareness of the other.

Long before I knew what was happening, I was being offered a deep trust. By opening their homes and their hearts to me, in sharing their private personal and sacred thoughts with me, countless individuals in India have consciously and unconsciously made me an emissary. I understand now that I can serve as a bridge between two cultures. I have long felt the deep need to set aright the extraordinary imbalance of Western opinions of India. We often base our views of the sub-continent on sensationalized media reports that focus on India's inequalities, injustices, and eccentricities without attempting to portray her strengths. As in most societies, great inequities exist and must be improved, but it is inappropriate to believe that these problems define the country and her people. Many of the negative conditions in India are indeed deplorable (overpopulation, social and economic disparity, and environmental pollution, among others); but it is essential to also recognize India's vitality, her statistics of positive change, and her remarkable agricultural, economic, and social improvements since independence. Projections assert that India will be a leading world power within the first few decades of the twenty-first century. It is time that we in the West begin to reeducate ourselves and reconsider our values. It is remarkable that as India modernizes, as her people grow into leading proponents of an innovative and contemporary world, their sense of religion and spirituality is not diminished. Hinduism, the world's third largest religion, accounting for one in every six human beings, is still as vital to the lives of the Indian people as it has ever been. It is a belief system in complete harmony with change, adaptation, modernization, and growth, and it affects every aspect of every day of most Hindu Indians.

For the average Hindu, the Divine is personal and approachable. The most common word describing worship is *darshan*, literally translated as "seeing and being seen by God." My own rich experiences in India during the past three decades have led me to a deep understanding of this process of "meeting God." In writing this book, I have attempted to convey the transformative intensity of worship in India as it evokes the heart as well as the mind, and as it involves the active use of all the senses. Although this work is based on field research and scholarship, I have chosen to focus my descriptions of daily and seasonal devotions more upon the way they impact individual Hindu devotees than upon scriptural or textual resources. Libraries are filled with books that richly describe the Hindu religious canon, but there are few that attempt to give a sense of the many ways that this religion permeates the daily lives of the people of India. Hinduism demands the active participation of all the senses. I have purposely simplified and condensed an extremely complex and diverse religion in order to clearly convey its commonalities. In doing so I hope not to offend by generalizations but to encourage the reader to delve further into Hinduism and the cultures of India. This book is intended to portray forms of spirituality that have distinctly evolved in the Indian subcontinent but that nevertheless may resonate in the lives of those of us living in other countries. Hinduism is a religion of strength, vitality, innovation, and balance. By opening our hearts and minds to its messages, we can enrich our own lives.

# Concepts of Hindu Devotion

ONE

A damp chill pervades the air as Amita wends her way down the dark street to the river. For warmth she pulls her sari about her head and adjusts her light wool shawl more tightly around her shoulders. Then she reaches down with both hands to pull her two young children along with her. They stumble sleepily as she guides them through the narrow passageways. Just above the river she stops quickly to buy a small lamp made of a curled dried leaf. In its center a daub of clarified butter holds a wick. The three sidle through the huddled bodies of unidentifiable figures and down the ancient stone steps that run as far as they can see along the river's edge, steps grooved through centuries of use. And then the black expanse of the river fills their gaze and they slip off their sandals and walk down the last steps into the icy cold water. The children are reluctant, their teeth chattering; their mother is determined, intent on fulfilling this ritual, which begins each day of her life.

First she takes her ten-year-old daughter, Meenu, and presses her down into the water. A bar of soap materializes from a plastic bag in her waistband, and she briskly scrubs Meenu's head and neck, arms and legs, reaching up under her clinging dress to wash her hips and torso. The girl then dunks quickly and clambers up the shore. Then Amita similarly washes Bablu, her seven-year-old son. He is cold, but uncomplaining. Finally, it is her turn to dip deeply into the river, wash herself while still dressed in yesterday's sari, and return to the bank to collect the children. Now they are clean and ready to greet the day.

All the while the sky has been lightening. Across the river the promise of sunrise turns the water from deep purple to rich blues tinged with orange. The shivering three step again into the water, which now seems warm compared to the biting air. Amita is immersed to her knees, Meenu and Bablu to their waists. Together they sing prayers to the Goddess

PRECEDING PAGES

VARANASI, UTTAR PRADESH

Women literally immersed in predawn prayer to Hinduism's most sacred river, the Ganges, viewed as the Goddess Ganga.

OPPOSITE

VARANASI, UTTAR PRADESH

Every morning of the year millions of Hindus rise early to bathe in a nearby river or pond and then pray to the rising sun.

Ganga, who is also the river. They visualize her magnificence, her nurturing presence as the Purifier and Mother of All Existence. With a match Meenu lights the small leaf lamp and gently floats it out before them. At that moment, the sun's first rays peek above the sandy horizon, and they begin singing to the Sun God, Surya, the Source of All Energy, the Great Provider. In acknowledging the two they also acknowledge the One, for in Hinduism the supreme deity is the absolute complement of opposites, of masculine and feminine, of dark and light, of wrong and right, of good and evil. By beginning each day in this way they attune themselves with the universe and validate their place in it. They are essential parts of a greater whole.

As the sun rises to warm the river and the ancient city crowded on its banks, Amita and her two children climb the stone steps back to dry land. Reaching into a shoulder bag that she had left on the shore, she pulls out dry, clean clothes for them all. First she deftly strips Bablu and helps him into a pair of shorts. Then she holds up her folded sari as a screen behind which Meenu quickly changes into a clean, dry cotton skirt and blouse, her school uniform. Finally, with rapid and remarkable dexterity, Amita wraps the dry sari around herself as she peels off her soaking underlayers, pleating, draping, and folding the outer garment until she is properly dressed. She then squats down on the river's edge and rubs all the wet clothes with a bar of soap, scrubbing them against the ancient stone steps and rinsing them in the water.

VARANASI, UTTAR PRADESH
Water symbolizes the sacred feminine, an equal half of all creation that should be honored daily.

Amita puts the laundry into her bag and the three climb back to the street that leads to their home. Once there, the clothes, cleaned by the sacred waters of Ganga, will be hung out to dry in the warmth of Surya, the sun. For in Hinduism the sacred and the mundane, the spiritual and the practical are in constant balance, the one providing context for the other. For Amita the day has begun as it will continue, honoring the Divine in acts of simple ritual.

As Amita and her children prayed on the banks of the Ganges River, all around them hundreds, thousands of others were beginning their day in similar fashion. The rituals of each were slightly different from those of his or her neighbor. Throughout India, millions use water in their daily prayers to the sun. But the ways these prayers are enacted are as varied as the participants because in Hinduism, alone of all the major religions in the world, there is no one right way. Hinduism is a religion of individuality. Many Hindus start their day praying while standing in water. Others pour water from vessels as the sun rises. Some may choose to worship at sunset, or at any other time. And not everyone worships Surya and Ganga. Many choose other forms of the Divine as their means of essential contact with the Absolute. But virtually all Hindus believe that the Absolute is the pure blend of opposites, neither masculine nor feminine. The focus and means of worship are many, but the process has a common thread. It acknowledges one of the fundamental principles of Hinduism: God is a universal force, indivisible and yet infinitely divisible, the one and the many, the perfect mixture of all facets of existence.

Literally, *Hindu* simply means "of India," a term devised by those outside the culture attempting to understand it. Many contemporary followers of this indigenous religion of India call it Sanatana Dharma. Hinduism is often said to be a religion of millions of Gods, and it is indeed a religion of diversity. But it is essential to understand that underlying all is the belief in the unity in one great God: the Absolute, often known as Brahman. Some Hindus believe that this Absolute is formless, a supreme cosmic force that cannot be completely known by humankind. Hindu philosophers state that existence as we know it is an illusion. The universe is relative, ever changing, whereas its source, the Absolute, is the only permanent thing, never changing. To truly reach the Divine we must divest ourselves of all physical attachments and open our minds and spirits to the great void. Most Hindus, however, believe in an Absolute that manifests itself and its powers through the Gods and Goddesses. By selecting one or more of these deities to worship, and by conducting rituals designed to facilitate contact with them, a Hindu devotee is striving to recognize his or her unity with the Absolute—like Amita and her children in their prayers to the masculine and feminine, God and Goddess, sun and river.[1]

India is a complex country. Throughout its several millennia of history, its many kingdoms, empires, invasions, and trading contacts have created unparalleled cultural diversity. For example, its people speak 325 languages expressed in more than two thousand dialects and twenty-five scripts. Each region has a

pronounced individual character: usually its own social and ethnic composition, language, climate, geography, agriculture, and industry. A recent government anthropological survey documents eighty thousand subcultures.[2] Each community has a specific and unique regional mythology and belief system, and every town and village has its own names for the Gods and Goddesses worshipped there. Although several centuries of theologians have identified the similarities of many of these individual deities and have urged that they be called by common names, such as Rama or Durga, regional personalities still exist.

With all of these individual perceptions and traditions, it is easy to understand why definitions of Hinduism have baffled so many Westerners. In fact, Hinduism is not one codified religion but a compilation of hundreds, perhaps thousands, of smaller belief systems. Today one of every six human beings living on our planet is a Hindu (of India's present population of almost 1 billion, 82 percent are Hindu). Statements are frequently made that Hinduism incorporates thousands or millions of Gods, but that number refers to the entire country, not to individual beliefs. In practice, each Hindu worships only those few deities that he or she believes directly influence his or her life.

**KUMBAKONAM, TAMIL NADU**

Hinduism is often misunderstood as a religion based on the worship of two primary male deities: Vishnu and Shiva; but most Hindus view the Divine as a complement of both masculine and feminine. In order to convey that concept, a common depiction of Shiva views him as Ardhanari: his right half is male, while his left half is female.

Hindus rarely proselytize; most respect the rights of others to their own beliefs. According to the tenets of Hinduism, all philosophies and belief systems are considered equally valid paths to salvation, and it is thought inappropriate to judge the choices of others. Exceptions to this attitude are found in politically motivated disturbances, such as the Hindu-Muslim or Hindu-Sikh riots of the twentieth century. Without political exploitation, Hindus usually live in close harmony with those of all religions.[3] Hindu children grow up learning to follow the tenets and customs of their parents, but in adolescence and young adulthood they are encouraged to make their own choices as to which primary Gods or Goddesses they find personally inspiring. Many Hindus continue to observe the rituals associated with the deity to whom the family has prayed for generations, but it is by no means unusual for a son or daughter to realize that his or her needs will be better met by focusing on a different deity and its corresponding rituals. Although as adults they will continue to practice many family rituals, they will also conduct their own private worship. To perform these rituals correctly, Hindus usually rely on the advice of respected religious teachers and priests. In most cases, Hindus who choose different deities still will retain the respect and goodwill of those who continue inherited traditions. In this way, one frequently finds husband and wife worshipping different principal deities. For example, a man might worship the God Shiva, while his wife, coming from a different birth family with different needs, prays to the God Krishna.

Their children, as they grow older, may observe the rituals of either or both parents, or the son might choose to worship, for instance, the Goddess Durga, and their daughter yet another manifestation of the Divine, Hanuman. The worship of different deities within a family does not negatively affect family equanimity.

No emphatic statement can be made about Hinduism that cannot be contradicted; it truly is a religion of opposite and complementary forces that embraces an extraordinary diversity. Three primary sects harmoniously coexist in India: the worshippers of Shiva, also known as Devi (the Creator and Destroyer of all Existence), the worshippers of Vishnu (the Protector or Preserver of the Universe), and the worshippers of Shakti (the Pervasive Feminine Principle, the Dynamic Power). Each of these deities is believed by their millions of devotees to be the

Supreme Personified Godhead.[4] Most Hindus, however, also believe that the universe functions by the symbiotic coexistence of all of these powers, each of which must be acknowledged in order to maintain balance. Those that consider themselves Shaivas, the disciples of Shiva, often still worship Vishnu and Shakti, while Vaishnavas, the adherents to faith in Vishnu, may still pray to Shiva and Shakti. Their allegiance to one primary deity does not deny the importance of their recognition and honoring of the rest. Furthermore, each sect has its own mythology, which includes complex substrata of incarnations and/or attendant deities and the subsequent texts, rituals, and social and cultural observances.

Many descriptions of Hinduism focus on the two most popular sects: the Shaivas and the Vaishnavas. Scholars often define the religion as centered upon the worship of the two male deities for whom these sects are named. In doing so, they misinterpret Hinduism. All Hindus recognize the feminine complement to a masculine God. In fact, the word for "power" in most Indian languages derives from the Sanskrit word *Shakti*, which means Divine Feminine energy.[5] A male deity's strength comes from his feminine consort. Vishnu is almost always shown accompanied by either one Goddess, Lakshmi, or two, Bhudevi and Shridevi. Shiva is incomplete without the Goddess Parvati. In fact, a common image of Shiva depicts the God as Ardhanari: the right half of the body is male, the left half is female. A devotee may choose to pray to only half of the manifestation of the Divine; but she or he will always be aware that the other half is of equal importance to the existence of all creation.

The concept of multiple deities can be overwhelming to an outsider. For the believer, the Absolute unmanifested Brahman has taken forms in order to govern specific aspects of existence and to provide direct and indisputable guidance to devotees. It is considered natural that as humans we respond to those deities that meet our individual needs. Some, such as Shiva, are demanding of a rigorous and disciplined life. Rama, one of the ten incarnations of Vishnu, is a leader and warrior whose qualities are justness and social balance. Krishna, another of Vishnu's incarnations, is linked to the heart and to salvation through love. The Goddess Durga is the embodiment of the feminine power of action, invoked as a decisive force to bring about change by vanquishing evil and restoring peace. Lakshmi is the feminine provider of wealth and prosperity, prayed to for the health and welfare of the family. Ganesha, one of the sons of Shiva, is beseeched at the beginning of any endeavor to bring about its success.

As they worship, almost all Hindus direct their prayers to several deities, either at once or individually, attuning themselves to those aspects of the divine essence that they find pertinent to their own needs. For example, each profession has a patron deity who, if properly honored, is believed to facilitate success. Craftsmen pray to Prajapati or Vishvakarma, the Progenitor and God of Creativity. Farmers pray to the Earth Goddess Bhudevi or Gauri for fertility and good harvests. Most shops have within them a shrine to the Goddess Lakshmi in order to attract prosperity. Teachers, dancers, and musicians honor Saraswati, the Goddess of Learning and the Arts. Soldiers might pray to Rama or Hanuman for might in battle, or to one of the many forms of Shakti (for example, Durga or Kali) for her supreme strength and undefeated power. A cook honors Annapurna, the Goddess of Culinary Arts. A pregnant woman may pray to the Goddess Parvati or the Goddess Mariamman to ensure a successful childbirth.

VARANASI, UTTAR PRADESH

Often the eyes are the most important part of a sacred icon. They facilitate that most essential climax of all worship: *darshan*, seeing and being seen by God. This brilliant red sculpture depicts Hanuman, the Monkey God who is the faithful messenger of Lord Rama.

## PUJA

*Puja* is the ceremonial act of showing reverence to a God or Goddess through invocation, prayer, song, and ritual. An essential aspect of puja for Hindus is communion with the Divine. The worshipper believes that with this contact she or he has established direct contact with the deity. Most often that contact is facilitated through an image: an element of nature, a sculpture, vessel, painting, or print. When the image is consecrated at the time of its installation in a shrine or temple, the deity is invited to invest the image with his or her cosmic energy. In the eyes of most devotees, the icon then becomes the deity, its presence reaffirmed by the daily rituals of honoring and invocation. Certainly most Hindus recognize that the magnitude of a God or Goddess is far greater than any image. Nevertheless, most also believe that divine power is so magnificent that it can be present anywhere in the world at any time. In other words, while one image of Shiva in a small town temple is believed by his devotees to be the God incarnate in stone, it is nevertheless consistent in Hinduism that every

other sculpture of Shiva in each of hundreds of thousands of shrines through-out the world also contains his divine presence and power. Many Hindu sages have remarked that very few are able to understand the abstract, formless essence of the Absolute. Most individuals, they state, need to approach God through images and with rituals specific to that deity, not so much because the deity requires it but because of the limitations of the devotee. They believe that humans need something concrete on which to focus in prayer. Hinduism ful-fills that need through innumerable manifestations. Although many images are exquisitely and elaborately fashioned by sculptors or painters, and, for the devout Hindu, artistic merit is important, it is secondary to spiritual content. Images are created as receptacles for spiritual energy; each is an essential link that allows the devotee to experience direct com-munion with the Gods.

The principal aim of any puja is this feeling of personal contact with the deity. *Darshan*, literally translated from Sanskrit as "seeing and being seen by God," is that moment when the wor-shipper is receptive to recognition by the God or Goddess. Darshan may be achieved in a variety of ways. It may be felt by an individual during his or her daily household pujas or medi-tations, when the contact is made alone. A person may experience darshan simply by viewing a particularly sacred sculpture or holy spot, perhaps during a pilgrimage or at a fes-tival. Or the individual may feel a special communication with the deity through the intervention of a priest during a strictly regulated temple ritual. Through whatever means it comes, darshan brings both peace and blessing to Hindu devotees, and through it, they believe, miracles can and do occur frequently.[6]

Hinduism is not in general a congregational religion. Its adher-ents worship singly or in small family units. Most sacred rituals take place in the home or in temples or shrines that may be vis-ited at any time from early morning until late night (in some parts of the country they may be closed for several midday hours). Unlike most other religions, Hinduism has no sermons. Priests are trained to act as liaisons with the Divine, learning the complex prescriptions of rituals that must be enacted precisely to show proper respect to the Gods and to facilitate darshan for the devotee. Learned priests and holy scholars may conduct discussions on sacred texts and philosophies, but these informal meetings are held outside the temple's sanctum. The closest parallel to Judeo-Christian services are *bhajanas*, in which followers of the Bhakti movement join to sing hymns and praises to their Lord Krishna, yet there still is no preaching as it is known in the West. Although anyone may

PRECEDING PAGES

BALIKONDALO, PURI DISTRICT, ORISSA

At least once each year almost all Hindus pray to the deities who pro-tect their professions and to the spirits of the tools they employ. Here, in front of a decorated potter's wheel and tools, a priest prays on behalf of the potter to Vishvakarma, the Progenitor and God of Creativity.

OPPOSITE

BHUBANESHWAR, ORISSA

Hinduism is not a congregational reli-gion. Although there are festival days during which it is deemed important to conduct worship, most devotees visit temples and shrines at their own convenience. This young woman is praying at a small shrine to the Goddess Santoshi-Ma.

worship at a temple at any time, there are auspicious times during the day when many people gather to perform pujas. The format is not congregational in the Judeo-Christian sense of the word; instead, each person lines up to get as close as possible to the image of the deity in order to have his or her darshan.

In spite of its focus on the individual, Hinduism still provides many occasions for group activities. Perhaps the most common are the numerous religious festivals held each year, usually joyous celebrations involving the entire community. Although some festivals are centered on the home, most involve special pujas at the appropriate nearby temples, which are thronged with devotees in their finest apparel. Others revolve around huge parades in which consecrated processional images of the deities are brought out once each year for public darshan by the elderly and infirm, who might not be able to visit the temple. Through pilgrimages a large group of devotees from one community can visit sacred spots in other parts of the country, gaining darshan and subsequent merit by performing pujas in these distant shrines and temples. Finally, recitations and reenactments of sacred stories are often held within or outside the temple, and they may be followed by discussions led by scholars and priests.

UCHHAPUR, PURI DISTRICT, ORISSA
Hindu society pivots on belief in the sanctity of the family: one's family is everything. Relationships between family members are of primary importance, and cherished values are passed down from generation to generation.

### DHARMA AND KARMA

Two underpinnings of Hinduism are *dharma* and *karma*. Dharma is translated as the supreme law of righteousness, the belief that there is an undeniable pattern to which all existence must adhere. Guidelines have been set down by the Gods and by the many sages, saints, and prophets in the form of ancient texts that prescribe the courses of action that one must follow in order to attain a balanced and fruitful life. The *Vedas*, compiled at least four thousand years ago,[7] are the four primary Hindu sources that form the basis of most orthodox rituals, in the same way that the Bible, the Torah, and the Q'uran do for Christianity, Judaism, and Islam. The *Upanishads* and *Puranas* are later compilations, the former discussing the fine points of theology and the latter further specifying the means of approaching both worship and the practical aspects of living. The two great epics, the *Ramayana* and the *Mahabharata*, provide paradigms in the form of detailed stories that illustrate appropriate choices in all aspects of life: education, marriage, child-rearing, family relationships, war, and death.[8] One of the most common phrases used by Indians today to describe their actions is "This is my duty." By duty they mean that an action is beyond choice; it is a part of dharma. By doing whatever is required they are fulfilling their roles as conscientious Hindus, attentive to the cosmic ebb and flow, the innate reciprocity that governs all existence.

Karma literally translates as action. It is the law of cause and effect based on the fundamental belief that every action creates an equal reaction, either obviously in the present or subtly in the future. Karma is the doctrine of absolute responsibility: everything we do or even think has repercussions. It is inextricably related to reincarnation, another basic belief of Hinduism. Hindus believe that the soul is eternal, reborn in countless forms. In each life we are different, given new choices that challenge our integrity. The way we conduct ourselves, our karma, governs the form and life into which we will next be born. The goal of a devout Hindu is to improve with each life until he or she will no longer have needs but, like the great sages and saints, will live to serve others, the one soul gradually merging with the greater soul that is the Absolute, Brahman. The doctrine of reincarnation has received criticism from practitioners of other philosophies, who state that it discourages initiative in India. In their opinion, many Hindus are so accepting of their status in life, their karma, that they are unwilling to make changes. Indeed, some do suffer from social apathy; but the sages state that this inertia is a misinterpretation of the principles of dharma. Appropriate behavior requires that one live by right thought and right action with heightened awareness of possible consequences. Dharma and karma underline the belief in ultimate culpability: man is defined by what he says and does. Optimally, this approach restrains initiative only when action is inappropriate.[9]

## VARNA

Varna refers to the traditional Hindu social order, known to outsiders as the caste system. Contemporary empathy for social equality has influenced the opinions of many people worldwide, causing them to condemn the caste system without attempting to understand its historical relevance. Varna was established in the *Vedas* to regulate and categorize society into four primary hereditary groups: the Brahmanas (priests), Kshatriyas (administrators and soldiers), Vaishyas (merchants), and Shudras (farmers, craftsmen, and laborers). Thousands of years of cultural expansion and resettlement have resulted in the further division of each of these varnas into countless subcastes (*jatis*). Conquered subjects and prisoners of war outside the primary society were forced into necessary but undesirable occupations: butchering animals, tanning leather, removing waste products. These hereditary positions were outside the four varnas (outcaste), and the people were considered "untouchable" because their labor made them susceptible to contagious diseases; contact with them was a health risk. Over the millennia the position of outcaste became canonized into an inviolable and socially discriminated position that is infamous worldwide. In some ways, however, the Hindu caste system may be seen as simply a feudal social order no worse or better than that of Europe or the rest of the world prior to the Industrial Revolution. It remained vital in India long after the relative dissolution of similar social organizations in other countries because of foreign imperial policy, not, as is often believed, because Indians were "naturally" reluctant to change. Indeed, until India came under the power of the British Empire, its cultures were considered by Western travelers and writers to be among the most advanced and forward looking. The British motto "Divide and Conquer" succeeded by inhibiting indigenous education and bolstering the caste system. Since Indian independence in 1947, prejudice and favoritism according to caste have been explicitly outlawed. Nevertheless, change is slow, and social inequality is as common in India as it is elsewhere.[10]

## BRAHMANAS

Millions of Brahmanas live in India today.[11] Although all are members of the varna that originally comprised only priests and their families, most today are involved in other occupations, such as farming, teaching, and business. Nevertheless, all priests in major Hindu temples are Brahmanas, whose education and training are hereditary. The priests are not celibate, and almost all have families. From early childhood Brahmanas intended to be priests are schooled in the scriptures and rituals necessary to perform pujas and other ceremonies correctly—to make an error in the recitation of ritual prayers could change the meaning of a ritual with unfortunate and sometimes disastrous consequences. Although the texts are published in copious and complex detail, priests pride themselves on memorizing them verbatim. For example, many Brahmanas (as well as laity) can recite perfectly the entire scriptures of the *Ramayana* and the *Mahabharata*, each as long as the Christian Bible. Brahmana priests believe that it is their karma to be born into a position to serve the Gods and humanity, and their dharma to preserve the integrity of Hindu traditions. By ensuring their own absolute purity in all matters (purity being more important even than spirituality), Brahmana priests maintain the continuity of the Hindu social order.

NAGARI, KANGRA DISTRICT, HIMACHAL PRADESH

Brahmana priests act as liaisons to the Divine in most temples. They are trained from childhood to conduct the rituals of worship that most appropriately facilitate contact between devotee and deity. Here a Brahmana prepares sacred substances for adorning a Linga, the aniconic image of Shiva.

While in most temples Brahmanas act as liaisons between devotee and deity, they are uninvolved with the many rituals that take place outside these sacred precincts. The lower castes often worship local deities in smaller community shrines that are administered by non-Brahmana priests. The position of a non-Brahmana priest in a small shrine may or may not be hereditary; such a priest's primary or part-time occupation is taking care of the shrine and facilitating pujas. In some cases the shrine is cared for by a group of community volunteers who divide their responsibility throughout the week, season, or year.

The primary purpose of most Hindu ritual is to bring balance and welfare to the family. Indian society is focused on the home, and the heart of every Hindu home is its shrine: the sacred space delineated for honoring and worshipping the Gods. While a particularly devout Hindu may visit a temple every day, others go there only to request a special favor of the deity or to fulfill specific vows. Temple worship requires the intervention of a Brahmana (always male), while in the home, contact between devotee and deity is direct. Brahmanas may be asked to officiate at the rituals involved with a certain sacred event, such as a wedding; but most household rituals are conducted by family members, usually the women. The pujas that take place in the household shrine are the foundation of all family actions and decisions—everything begins and ends there. The size and appearance of such a shrine is immaterial. It may be large and impressive, an entire room or a beautifully designed edifice; or it may be simply a tiny niche, or even just a row of religious prints pasted on a wall. Household shrines contain those images that pertain to the belief systems of the home's inhabitants, and it is not uncommon to find, in one household, several small individual shrines corresponding to the needs of members of the extended family.

OCHIRA, ALAPPUZHA DISTRICT, KERALA

In a sacred tree shrine, a young girl tips her head back so that her mother can mark her forehead with brilliant red vermilion, a common symbol of devotion.

SWAMIMALAI, TAMIL NADU

The household shrine is the center of family activity and is often cared for by the women of the home. Every morning and evening this schoolteacher prays to her personal and family deities in the shrine next to her kitchen. When the shrine is not in use, the wooden doors are closed to protect the sacred energy within.

The Hindu home, then, is a microcosm of one of the most unusual religions in the world. Its rituals are complex, but its essence is simple. It embraces the one and the many: a transcendent Absolute God and innumerable Gods and Goddesses. Hinduism is a religion of ultimate individuality and personal choice. Both good and evil are believed to be of God, and the purpose of most rituals is to maintain a balance between such opposites: creation and destruction, light and dark, masculine and feminine. For the Hindu, as every aspect of existence has a purpose, human meaning involves a fundamental sense of duty and of conscientious accountability. All individuals are considered part of the greater whole, which functions well only when each person fulfills his or her obligations. Within the Hindu home, as within broader society, that duty includes an intimate relationship with the sacred: from the first prayers to the river and to the rising sun, through all the tiny rituals that take place during the day, to the acknowledgment of the Divine at night. Spirituality pervades all existence.

*Approaching God:*
*Elements of Worship*

TWO

aving just shaved and bathed, Ramachandran wraps the three yards of his clean, freshly starched white cotton *dhoti* around his waist. He places a matching shawl over his shoulders, leaving his chest bare. He then steps into his rubber sandals and slips out the door of his home. Just in front of him, on the ground before the door, his younger sister has almost finished painting an elaborate *kolam*, a sacred design made with bleached rice flour. It is an activity that either she or his mother or his aunt performs every day of the year. As he walks carefully around it he admires the beautiful lotus she is creating. All around him the town is coming to life. He weaves among countless other kolams as he moves down the street, waving to his neighbor, an old man intent on milking his cow. Ramachandran is on his way to the temple.

Today is Tuesday, dedicated in southern India to the Goddess Mariamman, an embodiment of Shakti, the feminine power that conquers evil and heals disorder. When Ramachandran was sixteen he vowed that for the rest of his life he would fast every Tuesday. Now, ten years have passed, and he still maintains his vow. After his bath before sunrise, he drank a cup of tea and ate some rice cakes. For the rest of the day he will have only liquids, keeping his mind and body ritually pure in order to be a proper vessel for the Goddess's guidance. Although Ramachandran worships Mariamman every day in his household shrine, on Tuesdays he chooses to go to the temple. Usually he goes alone, although sometimes he is accompanied by other family members.

Near the temple the streets grow more crowded. From the stalls on each side hawkers call out their wares. Many sell the offerings that devotees take to the temple; others sell objects that are used in household shrines. Ramachandran purchases a

PRECEDING PAGES
OCHIRA, ALAPPUZHA
DISTRICT, KERALA

Every evening a non-Brahmana priest lights dozens of ghee lamps at the base of this sacred tree in order to honor the presence of the Divine.

OPPOSITE
SRI RANGAM,
TIRUCHIRAPPALLI, TAMIL NADU

Beneath one of the outer gates to a large temple, a street vendor sells garlands of flowers to be purchased as gifts for the Gods.

46

coconut and a packet of white camphor from the vendors that he frequents every week. He puts these into the small wicker basket that he carries, which already contains some bananas and the bright red hibiscus that he picked from the garden behind his home.

He approaches the temple gate, then leaves his sandals at the door and steps inside. Already he can hear the clanging of bells from the sanctum. Repeating the name of his Goddess—"Mariamman, Mariamman, Mariamman"— he joins the many other devotees who circle the central temple in a clockwise direction. Returning to the entrance, he pushes through the crowd to enter the temple itself. Inside it is dark and cool, filled with the thick, sweet smell of incense. Ramachandran joins the line of other male worshippers to the left of the inner sanctum. The women, wearing their brightest saris and flowers in their hair, line up opposite him. Children are on both sides. He reaches up to ring a bell suspended from the stone ceiling. Its strong tone clears his brain of extraneous thought and allows him to focus on the deity. By craning his neck he can just get a glimpse of the blackened stone image of the Goddess. She is dressed in a brilliant red sari, her neck covered with jewels and garlands of flowers, her head crowned with a diadem. The priest comes down the line of devotees collecting their offerings and returns to the sanctum. A curtain is drawn across the shrine for a few minutes of eager anticipation. Then, amid the clamor of bells, it is opened. The image of Mariamman is radiantly beautiful to him, newly adorned with fresh flowers, including two of Ramachandran's hibiscus. The priest waves a brass lamp lit with seven flames in a circular motion in front of the Goddess. Looking into the shrine, Ramachandran locks his eyes with those of the image: he has darshan

SRI RANGAM, TIRUCHIRAPPALLI, TAMIL NADU Another vendor sells camphor in small plastic packets that will be opened in the sanctum and lighted as invocations to the Divine. Each basket contains a lotus and a coconut to be offered inside the temple.

with the Goddess. At that moment he is filled with a feeling of well-being, of centeredness and belonging. His world is in balance.

The priest then brings out a tray of lighted camphor. All the worshippers place their hands quickly into the cool flame before touching them to their closed eyelids, symbolically opening their souls to communion with the Divine. On the same tray are little mounds of white sacred ash and red vermilion powder. With the fourth finger of his right hand, Ramachandran puts a dot of each in the center of his forehead between his eyebrows, the ash symbolizing purification through worship and the red symbolizing Shakti, the power of the Goddess. Then each person's basket of offerings is returned, some of its contents remaining as a donation to the temple, the rest blessed by the Goddess to be shared by the devotees. Ramachandran will take this *prashad* back to his family, so that they may partake in Mariamman's blessing.

BEDLA, UDAIPUR DISTRICT, RAJASTHAN

The primary image of the deity in a temple, such as this image of the Goddess Durga, may well have been worshipped in this spot for untold centuries. Each day she will be washed, adorned with sacred substances, dressed, bejeweled, and garlanded before she may be seen by the public.

The purpose of his weekly temple visit is over, and Ramachandran must return home quickly. Once there he changes out of his dhoti and shawl and puts on the black pants and white buttoned shirt of his work attire. After drinking only a glass of water he mounts his bicycle to ride to the shop where all day he repairs the computers that are so essential to maintaining business in contemporary India. As he solders the memory boards of broken mainframe hardware, he is content in the memory of his link with his Goddess and with the rituals that bring balance to his life.

L ike Ramachandran, many Hindus observe a weekly fast, the choice of day depending on the deity to whom they have vowed. Whether fasting or not, worshipping at home or in the temple, all Hindus begin their day by bathing. It is considered essential to approach a deity in as clean a manner as possible, both in body and in dress. Even the destitute will wash in a local reservoir or under a hand pump before approaching their household or community shrine. And those who live in the desert or in drought conditions will sprinkle a few drops of precious water on their faces, hands, and feet before beginning their pujas. Those who can afford it always put on fresh clothes in order to pray, the men either in simple traditional dress or contemporary pants and shirts, the women, depending on the region, in their cleanest saris or sets of tunic and *pajamas*, or blouses, skirts, and veils. Footwear is always taken off before entering a shrine—one symbolically removes the dirt of the outside world and enters the sacred space clean in body and in spirit.

Once the image of a deity has been consecrated, Hindus believe it to be the deity incarnate, no matter what its form. It may be an unaltered element of nature, such as a rock or tree or body of water; or it could be a stone- or wood-carving, a casting in brass or bronze, a painting, even a mass-produced print. The rituals of consecration for temple images are elaborate and closely prescribed through ancient texts and canons. The installation of images in the household shrine may be less complex, depending on the traditions of the caste, family, and community; but once the images are consecrated they are viewed as deities themselves and accorded profound respect. Images in temples and shrines are given the same treatment that would be shown to royalty or to a very honored guest. In a temple, this preferential treatment, called *upacharas*, is carried out by the chief priest and, possibly, his assistants; in the home it is most often the responsibility of the senior female, the matriarch.[1]

PRECEDING PAGES

MADURAI, TAMIL NADU

A teenage girl places flowers as the finishing touch on a sacred diagram that she has just drawn on the ground in front of her family's front door. This morning the painting is especially colorful to honor a sacred festival. Some days it is an intricate design crafted only in white, but the girl prides herself on painting a different decoration every day of the year as part of her invocations to the Divine.

OPPOSITE

MAMALLAPURAM, TAMIL NADU

Every morning this Brahmana priest bathes this ancient stone Linga, the aniconic image of Shiva, with several sacred substances, among them honey (shown here), sandalwood paste, milk, and a mixture of mashed fruit. In performing this action he demonstrates his great reverence for the God.

The first thing every morning, the image is gently awakened. Then it is bathed in holy water that comes from the Ganga (the Ganges River, which is also viewed as a Goddess) or from another sacred body of water. (There are many sacred rivers, streams, and springs in India.) Whatever its source, any water used in a shrine is considered mystically transformed into Ganga. After the image's initial bath it is anointed with substances believed to enhance its purity. (Prints or paintings, for obvious reasons, cannot receive daily applications of liquids. They are instead cleaned carefully and may be adorned with sacred powders or garlands of flowers.) Sculptures are first anointed with one substance, then rinsed with holy water; a second substance is applied, and again the sculpture is washed with water before the third application, and so on. These materials vary according to local traditions but often include honey, milk, yoghurt, sandalwood paste or turmeric, coconut water, a mixture of five fruits (*panchamrita*), and sacred ash (*vibhuti*). Once cleaned and anointed, the image is dressed in garments befitting its gender and station: a dhoti and shawl, or a sari or skirt and veil. It will then be adorned with jewelry (bangles, necklaces, nose rings, and a crown), depending on the "wealth" that it has acquired over the years as gifts from devotees. Finally it will be garlanded with flowers. This bathing and anointing ceremony is usually conducted in private. Public viewing is considered indiscreet, and invasive to the deity. The image may be seen by others only when it is properly dressed and adorned. Few Westerners recognize that the manner in which Hindu sculptures are most often exhibited in museums, galleries, and private collections both inside and outside India is considered disrespectful by many Hindus. The images may be beautiful in elemental form and design, but without their ritual apparel and adornment their display is thought inappropriate.[2]

**BHUBANESHWAR, ORISSA**

During rituals of worship every morning and evening, this image of the Goddess Santoshi-Ma is adorned with fresh flowers. When she is bejeweled and surrounded by flowers, her divine beauty is said to be so overwhelming that her devotees are overcome with rapture. Santoshi-Ma is believed to bring good luck and good health to her many devotees.

Hindus chant prayers and songs of praise to the deity during all the ceremonies of preparation, as well as during the puja itself. Many of these prayers (*shlokas*) are derived from the *Vedas* and have been recited in this precise form for many thousands of years. Others were collected or written by sages and saints in the past two millennia.[3] It is considered essential that shlokas be repeated precisely and with proper reverence. Hindus believe that the very name of a God or Goddess has magical properties, as do many other sacred words and verses. The cadence, quality, pitch, and vibration of a voice may pierce through the illusion of the material world and speak directly to God. In fact, many texts state that the Absolute, Brahman, is pure sound. Most classical Indian music is considered sacred, and fine musicians are treated as divinely inspired and are sometimes even regarded as saints, for through the magic of their voices and instruments they enable the listener to experience darshan. The tonal purity of bells ringing during a puja shatters the devotee's mundane train of thought and makes him or her directly receptive to the miracle of divine presence.

## DIVINE GIFTS

Hinduism revolves around the concept of reciprocity: a devotee's life is enhanced by the gifts he or she bestows. Both religion and hereditary society are based on this principle.[4] In a belief system that separates the unknowable Brahman into individually personified Gods and Goddesses, this exchange is essential. Most Hindu pujas involve expressions of thankfulness through the

symbolic offering of gifts to the deity, usually in the form of food and flowers. The type of offering depends on the financial ability of the devotee as well as the climate, season, and local tradition. Those living in wet, tropical areas might offer rice, bananas, and fresh fruits, while those in drier environments may give breads or sweets made of wheat or millet, or simple pellets of sugar. People in northern India prefer to give garlands of marigolds and roses, while in the south devotees offer more exotic flowers, such as jasmine, tuberoses, and hibiscus. Lotuses are highly valued as sacred gifts everywhere in India. Flowers are used to adorn the image of the deity, and food is placed in close proximity to it. During the puja rituals the deity is believed to symbolically consume the food. In doing so, his or her sacred energy seeps into the flowers and the remaining food, transforming them with vibrant divine power.

Many of the items donated to shrines are purchased in markets just outside or even within the temple compound. Florists sell individual blooms and garlands of flowers strung together by hand, and fruit sellers provide coconuts, bananas, and other produce. Confectioners display varieties of sweets and cakes, all to be given to the Gods. Other vendors peddle incense and camphor. Many cater primarily to the needs of household shrines, stocking their stalls with framed and unframed prints of painted portraits of the principal deities being worshipped inside the temple, as well as those of many other Gods and Goddesses that might be of interest to devotees. Brass shops carry not only lamps, incense burners, trays, and water vessels but also metal sculptures of popular Gods and Goddesses; other vendors sell the brocaded and embroidered costumes and miniature jewelry for these household images.

HARIDWAR, UTTAR PRADESH

Outside almost every temple are market stalls selling the objects required for worship either within the temple or in household shrines. Here a vendor of brass sells containers for sacred substances, lamps, incense burners, cymbals, bells, chains, frames, and sculptures of deities.

Certain occasions may require significant gifts to the Gods. The annual festival of one's patron deity may be an auspicious time to give something extra to the temple or shrine. Rituals that herald important life-changing events, such as birth, coming of age, or marriage, often involve the donation of presents to the family's temple. When a devotee prays for a specific boon from a deity—for example, the healing of a disease, success in a new project, or a raise in income—she or he promises to give a gift to the God or Goddess if the wish is granted. The quality and value of the gift depends on the financial capabilities of the donor. A common offering is a new garment for the image, often a cotton or silk sari or dhoti. Women may offer their own jewelry: glass, silver, or gold bangles, or gold or silver bracelets, anklets, earrings, necklaces, or rings. Wealthy individuals might commission fine jewelry, such as a crown or diadem, or perhaps even silver or gold coverings for a part of the body of the image. Terracotta sculptures are given by the poor to community shrines, although rarely to large temples. Typically these sculptures, ordered from local potters, represent those animals (horses, cows, or elephants) that tradition states are of particular interest to the deity. Many believe that the sculptures are transformed into their real counterparts in the spirit world for the deity's own use.[5]

Once the deity is suitably prepared for worship, the puja begins. Fire is an essential part of all Hindu rituals. Lamps (*deepas*) are lighted during a puja and waved clockwise in front of the image with the right hand, first around its head, then around its central portion, and finally around its feet. The left hand of the priest or person conducting the puja usually holds a small bell that is rung continuously while the lamp is being waved. Fire was worshipped in ancient India as the God Agni, and today fire is a primary symbol of divine energy. In lighting the flame in front of the image the devotee acknowledges the sacred supremacy of the God or Goddess. Various vegetable oils may be used in deepas, but the most auspicious fuel is *ghee*, or clarified butter. Most lamps are brass, and many are sculpted with sacred symbols relevant to the deity being worshipped. Camphor, known locally as *karpura*, is processed from the pitch of the camphor tree. When lighted, it has the unique property of creating a bright, cool flame that leaves no residue or ash. It is usually placed in a flat tray known as an *arati*. After being waved in front of the image, the arati is customarily brought close to the devotees so that they may put their hands into the fire and then touch their eyelids or the tops of their heads with their fingertips, an action with great symbolic value. The fragrant flame represents the brilliant presence of the deity. Contact with the fire is believed to purify and elevate the devotee's soul, allowing it to merge with the magnificence of the Divine; at the same time, the energy of the Absolute unknowable deity is transformed and channeled into palpable connection with the devotee. The arati puja and the darshan (the moment of visually recognizing and being recognized by God) are the most important acts in Hindu worship.

THANJAVUR, TAMIL NADU

Painted terracotta sculptures of children, devotees, and body parts are sold in a temple market to be purchased and placed near the image of a deity to remind him or her of specific prayers for aid.

PATNA, BIHAR

Simple clay lamps hold wicks fueled by ghee. Lamps are lighted in almost every Hindu ritual as symbols of transformation through contact with the Divine.

The arati is usually directly followed by the dispersion of water to the worshipper. A small brass container of holy water blessed by the deity is brought out of the sanctum. A spoonful is poured into the cupped right hand of the devotee, who drinks it and then rubs the remaining drops through his or her hair, thereby melding both the inside and outside of the body with the essence of the Divine. It is again an acknowledgment of the complement of opposites, the two primary elements: fire (masculine) and water (feminine), like the early morning prayers to the river and the rising sun.[6]

According to ancient Indian philosophy, the human body is divided into seven vortexes of energy, called *chakras*, beginning at the base of the spine and ending at the top of the head. The sixth chakra, also known as the third eye, is centered in the forehead directly between the eyebrows and is believed to be the channel through which mankind opens spiritually to the Divine.[7] At the end of each puja ceremony the devotee marks this chakra with sacred powder, usually either *kumkum* (vermilion) or vibhuti, or with a paste made of clay or sandalwood as a symbol and reminder of the darshan. The mark, or *tilak*, is a public proclamation of one's devotion and may identify a specific spiritual affiliation. Most common is a simple dot of bright vermilion that symbolizes the Shakti of the deity. Worshippers of Vishnu use white clay to apply two vertical lines joined at the base and intersected by a bright red streak. The white lines represent the footprint of their God while the red refers to his consort, Lakshmi. Devotees of Shiva customarily draw three horizontal lines across their brows with vibhuti, symbolizing the three levels of existence and the three functions of their Lord as Creator, Preserver, and Destroyer of all existence. A married woman in some parts of India may be identified by the vermilion used in her tilak and in the part of her hair. Contrary to popular belief outside of India, the *bindi*, or beauty mark, that modern Indian women and girls put on their foreheads has no other contemporary significance, although it evolved from these symbolic tilaks. It does not refer to caste, community, or marital status.

MANARASHALA, ALAPPUZHA
DISTRICT, KERALA

Almost all Hindu rituals of worship include the ceremonial placing of each devotee's hands in fire, symbolizing the cleansing of the soul and the lifting of the spirit in devotion. The flames are created by lighted camphor, a substance that burns cool and leaves no residue.

After the symbolic purification with fire, the drinking of holy water, and the marking of the third eye, the final act in most pujas is the return to the devotee of some of the flowers and the newly blessed food, called *prashad*. In the household, all the prashad will be consumed by family members. Some of the food remains in the temple as payment to the priests who facilitate the rituals, while the remaining prashad is taken home and eaten. Hindus believe that the ingestion of prashad fills them with the divine energy of the deity to whom they have prayed, in the same way that Christians believe that by partaking of the bread and wine in holy communion they accept the spirit of Christ into their bodies. While pujas may be made either before or after meals, depending on family tradition, all food that is cooked in the home must first be symbolically offered to the Gods before it is eaten. In the strictly traditional home the cook will never even taste the food while it is being prepared, as that would alter the purity of the offering. Consequently, all food cooked in these homes becomes prashad. The kitchen is therefore considered a sacred space that should not be violated by uncleanness or by impure actions, words, or thoughts.

# The Soul of Family:
# Worship in the Home

For Usha, the morning begins early. She is up long before sunrise to bathe in the pond not far from her home. The night before she had covered the exterior front walls of her house with a mixture of mud and cowdung to create a fresh canvas on which to paint. Now, using a stone mortar and pestle, she grinds freshly harvested rice into flour and mixes it with water to make a white paste. She reaches into a basket lying at her side, picks up her newborn baby girl, and wraps her in a length of old sari, which she ties into a sling at her chest. Usha then calls to her eight-year-old daughter, Neela, to bring her younger brother, little Arjuna, and they all go out the courtyard door to the street. The mother dips a homemade brush into the rice mixture and begins to rapidly paint the walls with sinewy vines, flower petals, birds, and animals. Her daughter divides her time between keeping Arjuna out of mischief and helping Usha to draw some of the less complicated patterns and to fill in others. The designs they create are symmetrical and yet free form, flowing from one shape to the next, transforming the entire thatched mud house into a personal expression of sensuous beauty. The wall is often repainted with sacred designs throughout the year, declaring to the Gods themselves and to all passersby the devotion of the members of this household.

While Usha is painting, her husband, Alok, barefoot and dressed in his white dhoti, approaches the elaborately sculpted planter that stands directly in front of the house. It contains a bronze-leafed bush of *tulasi*, an Indian species of basil worshipped throughout the country as an incarnation of the Goddess Lakshmi. In his hands Alok carries the objects for this first puja of the day: a brightly polished brass water pot, a clean strip of red cloth, and a garland of marigolds. He walks clockwise around the plant three times while quietly chanting prayers to the Goddess. He then removes the dusty red cloth he had wrapped

PRECEDING PAGES
DHUNDALI, JODHPUR DISTRICT, RAJASTHAN

A girl rings a bell and lights a lamp to the local Goddess Kalka in front of her family's household shrine sculpted in clay bas-relief.

OPPOSITE
UCHHAPUR, PURI DISTRICT, ORISSA

A farmer's wife paints her walls with decorations dedicated to Lakshmi, the Goddess of Abundance and Prosperity. When she is properly beseeched with prayers and beautiful paintings, Lakshmi is believed to fill the home with her protective spirit, keeping away misfortune.

66

around the plant's roots the day before and pours water over the bush, all the while intoning Lakshmi's names and attributes. Gently wrapping the fresh cloth around her base, he hangs the garland in her upper limbs and carefully shakes the stem. Just three tulasi leaves fall with this action. He thanks the Goddess, raises the leaves to his forehead, and carries them into the house.

As the sun rises over the outlying rice paddies, Usha finishes the painting and returns with her children to the courtyard. There the mother and daughter ladle water from large terracotta pots onto one another's hands and onto the face, hands, and feet of the little boy, and then they straighten all their clothes. The baby is put back into her basket. All the while Alok's mother has been preparing food over a cowdung fire in the small kitchen shed in one corner of the courtyard. She has puffed rice and sweetened it with molasses, has fried spicy cakes of lentil flour, and has arranged plates of fresh fruit and flowers. All of these offerings are carried to the tiny room next door, the room that contains the household Gods and Goddesses, the true center of the home.

The shrine itself is simple. A small raised platform holds the primary household images, although they are hard to identify beneath the tired blossoms of yesterday's offerings. Usha, as the family's leading female, sits to the left of the platform and conducts the puja. Her husband and her widowed mother-in-law sit on each side of her, while Neela and Arjuna face the shrine from the front. After an initial prayer Usha removes the faded flowers and tiny garments from the images to reveal in the center a small stone image of the hereditary family God, Krishna, playing his flute, along with a brass sculpture of his consort, Radha. To the right is a stone sculpture of the Sun God, Surya, and to the left a bronze image of Hanuman, the Monkey God. In the foreground are two *salagramas*, the

black fossilized ammonite shells that are common symbols of Vishnu. On the wall above these images is a framed and garlanded photograph of Alok's deceased father, as well as several framed and unframed prints of Gods and Goddesses, some emblazoned with advertisements for nearby businesses.

First Alok puts one tulasi leaf under his tongue and passes the other two to his wife and mother that they might do the same. Then Usha takes the same brass pot and pours holy water over each image, using her right index finger to rub them clean. As her mother-in-law hands her fresh garments, she dresses each image, chanting prayers to each as she does so. She puts a dot of brilliant vermilion on the foreheads and cardinal points of each image, as well as on her father-in-law's picture and on the prints on the wall. Finally she places fresh marigolds and hibiscus blooms on each sculpture and a new small garland over the photograph. All are now ready for the main puja.

PADMAPODA, PURI DISTRICT, ORISSA

The walls of this small household shrine to the God Vishnu are painted with sacred designs: pots with coconuts, a common Hindu symbol of welcome, and elephants, which honor Lakshmi. Inside, a small wooden platform holds freshly dressed household images crowned with flowers.

The ritual itself is straightforward. The plates of cooked food and fruit are held up as offerings to the deities. Alok then lights cubes of camphor in a small arati dish, which he gives to his wife. As the family members join together to sing prayers to the assembled deities, Usha takes the arati in her right hand and waves it in a clockwise circular motion in front of each image while with her left hand she rings a small brass bell. In attuning their spirits to the presence of all the deities, each of the adults concentrates on opening her or his heart to darshan with a chosen deity. After the arati plate is passed around so that each person may place his or her hands into the flame, the ceremony is finished. The newly blessed food is taken into the courtyard to be eaten while the grandmother stokes up the fire to make tea and breakfast. The spirits of home and family have been acknowledged, honored, and met with, and now the day's activities may begin.

The rituals of worship differ in each Hindu home. Those of the same sect in a specific region will have similarities, but there are variations according to individual, family, and affinity. Some customs of a particular sect are observed throughout India, while others are unique to a single locality. The rituals of the members of different sects even within the same community may bear little similarity to one another, while those in distant states may seem completely different. Nevertheless, most involve the washing and adorning of images, the offering of food and distribution of prashad, the use of arati and bells, and darshan with the chosen deities.

Virtually all Hindus, regardless of age, sex, race, subculture, creed, caste, social standing, or occupation, are diligent in their practice of daily devotion. The choice of rituals, such as those observed by Usha and her family, may be individual, but they nevertheless permeate every aspect of each Hindu's day. In spite of this adherence to tradition, India is a modern country. Almost every person throughout the subcontinent uses some form of contemporary technology and is aware of the advances promoted through innovative education. Satellite television, mass media, electronic music, new fashions, and labor-saving gadgets have pervaded every community and are creating a constant challenge for all Indians. Increased urbanization, an improved economy, and a burgeoning better-educated middle class have created new attitudes. Previously rigid social and occupational restrictions are being relaxed, more women are working outside the home, and more of the young are being allowed to voice their marital choices. And yet even the most contemporary Hindu usually maintains the sacred rituals that govern daily and seasonal life. Hinduism may have its roots in an archaic society, but it has always adapted to the social and technological changes confronted by its devotees. Today the observance of household pujas is of equal importance to the neurosurgeon and the farmer, the nuclear physicist and the fisherman, the computer technician and the weaver. Although many twentieth-century Westerners tend to view the practice of religion as incompatible with living in the modern world, and while membership in many churches and synagogues dwindles each decade, Hinduism is as strong as ever. Indeed, in India it is vital to contemporary life.[1]

In traditional Christian and Jewish theology, only human beings have souls, a belief that is sometimes expanded to include animals. Hindus, however, believe that every aspect of creation has an individual spirit. Every blade of grass, every rock, every tree, every body of water has a spiritual essence worthy of respect.

PRECEDING PAGES
MOTISINGHKILOKIDHANI, JODHPUR
DISTRICT, RAJASTHAN

A camel herder prays to the Goddess Lakshmi and the God Ganesha in the bas-relief shrine inside his home in the remote Thar Desert. For the Hindu, any consecrated image may serve as a vehicle for divine energy. Thus a poster is no less valuable than a fine painting or sculpture.

OPPOSITE
BANTALIGRAM, PURI DISTRICT,
ORISSA

Inside her shrine room an elderly woman, the mother of a school-teacher, meditates on sacred verses proclaiming the virtues of her primary deity, Vishnu.

Natural elements that are used by humankind, such as the wood carved for the handle of a tool, or the metal forged into a blade, or the clay fashioned into a vessel, combine their innate spirits with the energy believed to be put into the object by the craftsperson. The result is a blend of the spirits of both the original substance and that of the human who transforms it. If the object is then used over a period of time, the power of its spirit is thought to increase. If it is used in ritual or in puja, it is imbued with the energy of the Divine: it becomes sacred.

A home in India is considered a sacred entity. It contains all of the individual elements that go into its construction—all of the timbers, tiles, stone, and hardware that give it its final shape. Each of these elements has its own individual spirit, which is blended by the builders into a dwelling that then contains all of the sacred and mundane energies and activities of its inhabitants. If a home is lived in for generations, as most in India are, then it is believed to hold within it not only the spirits of the present inhabitants but also those of its previous occupants, usually ancestors. All of this spiritual energy must be acknowledged and honored through daily and/or seasonal rituals.

NAGARI, KANGRA DISTRICT, HIMACHAL PRADESH

The home of a middle-class farmer.

UMRAJ, SATARA DISTRICT, MAHARASHTRA

The home of an impoverished fisherman.

## KULADEVATA

The deity that is worshipped as the protector of home and the particular family and clan is called the *kuladevata*. This God or Goddess is often directly associated with the house itself and is viewed as a composite of all the individual spiritual energies within it. It defines the essence of the Hindu family, the specific history of births, activities, and deaths, and of all the complex interrelations that make that family individual. Innumerable ceremonies and rituals are enacted to ensure the purity of the kuladevata. A home should never be violated with negativity, particularly by outside forces. Special prayers and pujas are designed to remove unwanted energy, to cleanse a home after a violent episode or a death. Even small intrusions from the outside world may be viewed as creating an imbalance that must be rectified through rituals.[2]

Household shrines are as varied in form as the innumerable homes in which they are found. Some are rooms, large or small; others are cupboards, niches, or shelves; still others are composed simply of a row of religious posters on a wall. All are a direct mean for meeting and honoring the Gods.

Similarly, a family's relationships are considered sacred. Great deliberation is given to marital choices. Most Hindus are patrilineal and endogamous, which means that brides always marry into a community other than their own, although the bridegroom is usually someone from the same varna and jati (caste and subcaste) and the same religious sect. The majority of Hindus still observe the tradition of living in extended families: one large house contains the parents, their unmarried daughters, all their sons, their daughters-in-law, and their grandchildren. Consequently, the dynamics of a family are always

77

changing as marriageable girls leave the home and new brides enter it. A delicate balance must be maintained by the inhabitants of the house. Brides must be chosen with particular care so that they are both compatible with other family members and will respect the rituals of the family. They must bring honor to the kuladevata.[3]

The identity of the kuladevata depends entirely on a family's individual history. The household reveres a specific form of God or Goddess unique to their clan. Their forebears have lived for untold centuries in the same community and have passed down prescribed rituals that must be enacted in order to maintain balance within the home and family. But India is also a subcontinent of constant change that has always been subject to the movement and resettlement of its populations. When a Hindu changes primary residence, the kuladevata is believed to remain in the hereditary household. Hindus make periodic visits to the ancestral home, not only to visit family members but also to reestablish contact with the household deity. For this reason, second-, third-, and fourth-generation urban Indians almost always keep in touch with the village or town from which their paternal ancestors migrated. For example, when asked where he comes from, a resident of Delhi or Madras will most often state his ancestral community rather than the city of his domicile. He is still linked to the family deity: it remains the spirit of his origin, his lineage, and his present identity.

Some Hindu subcultures provide a method of transferring this sacred energy to a new location through a special ritual. The spirit of the kuladevata is requested to permeate the water in a clay vessel. This terracotta pot, now a vehicle for the kuladevata's divinity, is then taken to the new home and installed in the household shrine to be honored in daily pujas. Successive generations may continue to worship this kuladevata in its vessel form, or its spirit may be further transferred into another image: a sculpture, painting, or print subsequently viewed as the household deity. Hinduism, as has been discussed, is unique among major religions in providing a vehicle for change in beliefs. If a devotee is inspired, for example, by witnessing a miracle or by the teachings of an influential guru, he or she may convert to a different sect, to focus on a different primary deity. The change may affect the entire family, so that the identity of the kuladevata also alters. Consequently, some families worship household deities that are unique, while others worship personalized forms of pan-Indian Gods or Goddesses.

In southern India, for example, a popular incarnation of the God Vishnu, known as Balaji or Venkateshwara, is associated with a specific temple on a sacred mountain in Tirupati in Andhra Pradesh. Every day of the year an average of thirty thousand pilgrims visit this temple for darshan with Balaji. He is called the Bestower of Boons because he can be approached easily by anyone and usually grants his devotees' wishes. Balaji is also worshipped as a kuladevata in many homes throughout the south, and in each home he is synonymous with the family's identity. Although he is acknowledged in daily prayers, he may or may not be the primary deity of household members. However, it is essential that, as kuladevata, Balaji be prayed to first on all occasions that particularly affect the family—for instance, at *samskara* ceremonies, the sacraments that mark stages in a person's life: conception, birth, coming of age, betrothal, marriage, and so forth.[4]

## ISHTADEVATA

In most Hindu homes the images of all the deities being worshipped by different members of the household are contained in one shrine. Some large buildings are subdivided into several sections so that each of the nuclear units within the greater extended family may have its own living space. While the kuladevata is generally housed within the principal shrine, belonging to the parents or to the family of the oldest brother, each of these smaller units may also have its own shrine. Every Hindu worships his or her own *ishtadevata,* the deity or deities chosen by the devotee for personal reasons. One's ishtadevata is the direct manifestation of the unmanifested Brahman, a form of the Divine that resonates with the individual and gives guidance in the complex and confusing world of the Hindu.

ALLAHABAD, UTTAR PRADESH

The widowed mother in an upper-middle-class home spends up to several hours each day in puja in her shrine. Photographs of her guru, Satya Sai Baba, share the place of honor with images of the family's deities.

The choice of ishtadevata is an intimate decision based on one's own spiritual experience. Many Hindus choose to worship the Gods and Goddesses that were the primary focus of their parents. They are familiar with these deities; they have grown up with their worship and have experienced the benefits of their pujas. Some decide that their particular natures or requirements respond to different facets of the Divine. Other Gods or Goddesses fulfill their specific needs. A new bride brings into the household her own heritage, which may include an entirely different ishtadevata from that of her husband. Part of her duty in her new marriage is to honor her new family's kuladevata, but the worship of her own ishtadevata is inviolate. For example, Krishna and Radha are the kuladevatas of Usha and Alok's family. Alok, like his father before him, worships Hanuman as his ishtadevata, but Usha's personal deity is Surya, the Sun God. Usha grew up in a village close to a magnificent temple to the sun and had long been attracted to this celestial deity. Their children,

as they come of age, may choose to worship either deity or may be influenced by a mentor or friend to pick another God or Goddess, or even an entirely different sect, for their own personal devotion.

Alok's brother and his family live in the same house as Alok, but on the other side of a partition that divides the central courtyard. They are fortunate that they are not overcrowded in this home. In India, ten or more individuals may live in a single room. The economy of space in such dwellings dictates that there be little or no furniture. Everyone sleeps on the floor, and during the day bedding is stored in the rafters or in a corner to make room for activities. In these houses of the poor the shrine may consist simply of a row of poster prints on the wall, or perhaps a small niche built into the wall that contains prints or a few simple images. A larger home may have a more elaborate niche, or perhaps a three-dimensional wooden shrine to contain the family's deities and accoutrements for puja. Some shrines are built into closets or small separate rooms. The homes of the upper middle class and wealthy are often designed with entire large rooms devoted to household pujas, while aristocrats and royalty may have their own temples away from the main house, in the manner that their counterparts in Europe would have had family chapels, churches, or even cathedrals. Whatever its size, the shrine holds the images of the family's kuladevata and ishtadevatas, as well as the objects and substances required for pujas. Its grandeur reflects the wealth of the householder but is otherwise irrelevant for the primary purpose of puja: darshan. Although a wealthier family may be able to afford a more elaborate image—one sculpted or painted by a fine artist and adorned with gold-brocaded silks and real jewelry—Hindus believe that all consecrated images are equally valuable as receptacles for divine energy. For its sacred purpose, a commercial print is no less important than a finely cast bronze or carved stone sculpture.

In response to India's rapid population growth (almost tenfold in just two centuries) millions of new homes have been constructed, each with its own shrine. While the original family homestead may still contain the images that have been worshipped for generations, most of these new shrines require fresh images, which are purchased in temple markets and consecrated in special rituals of invocation. The new sculpture, painting, or print is invited as an honored guest into the home with great celebration. It is bathed, dressed, and adorned in the best manner that the family can afford. The divine energy of the specific deity is asked to enter and transubstantiate the image, changing it from a

*LOL*

PRECEDING PAGES
CHENNAI (MADRAS), TAMIL NADU
Weddings are among Hinduism's most sacred ceremonies, and the rituals can last for several days. Although a ceremony can take place anywhere, it is always centered around a sacred fire. Here, with a priest's directions, a Tamil Brahmana bridegroom gives offerings of fruit and flowers to his bride, thereby showing that he honors the Goddess within her.

OPPOSITE
SOUTHERN INDIA
Only after an image has been properly cleaned, dressed, and adorned is it considered prepared for worship. Here, inside the inner sanctum of a palace, a Mukha Linga, the image of Shiva, is ready to be worshipped by the royal family.

82

This rock crystal Linga — being washed with sacred substances and honored with a flame — was given in the eighth century to a southern Indian royal family by the preeminent Hindu saint, Shankaracharya. Shown here with its accompanying images of the God Ganesha and the Goddess Parvati, it is considered to be the pivot of sacred energy for the entire kingdom. It has never before been viewed by anyone outside the family. After being bathed, the crystal Linga is placed in a brass box, the top of which is a brass Linga surmounted by a hood of snakes. Once dressed and adorned with flowers, it is honored with incense and camphor and readied for prayers. Both the head priest (shown here) and the Maharajah had visions that this process be allowed to be photographed for this book, but a request was made that the exact location not be stated.

man-made object into the God or Goddess incarnate. Then prayers, mantras, and songs are intoned as gifts of flowers, fruits, and specially cooked sweet and salty food are proffered. Lamps are lighted, bells rung, and arati waved as the new image is welcomed into the home to become a constant residing presence.

The Hindu year is punctuated by innumerable other customs for honoring the deities that are believed to protect the family. Many involve the annual construction of temporary shrines to specific deities with entire arrays of consequent rituals (see Chapter 7). Others, such as the worship and use of tulasi, are more permanent. Many legends describe the origin of tulasi, which usually is viewed as an incarnation of the Goddess Lakshmi, the wife of Vishnu. Some say that she was cursed by a jealous deity and turned into a plant. Others tell that Vishnu himself transformed the Goddess into the herb, which is considered essential to the health of humankind. He hoped that her devotees, by using her leaves daily, would be reminded of her divine virtue. Tulasi is used as a primary ingredient in many traditional Indian medicines, particularly those used to cure blood and skin diseases. Ancient treatises extol its properties as an antidote for poisons, a curative for kidney disease and arthritis, a preventative for mosquito and insect bites, and a purifier of polluted air. The sacred texts dictate that all worshippers of Vishnu ingest at least one tulasi leaf every day as a part of their household pujas. Consequently, millions of homes in India grow sacred basil in their gardens or in small planters. Most of these vessels are unadorned clay pots; some, such as the one cared for daily by Alok, are elaborately sculpted to represent small temples to the Goddess.[5]

BALIKONDALO, PURI DISTRICT, ORISSA

Every worshipper of the God Vishnu and the Goddess Lakshmi (that is, hundreds of millions of Hindus) keeps a planter of tulasi outside the home; the leaves are used in daily pujas. The plant is viewed as the Goddess herself and is believed to have many healing properties.

When Usha paints her home before her morning puja, she enacts a tradition practiced by women everywhere in India. Most paintings are created as invocations to the deities of protection, often the Goddess Lakshmi. The form, style, substance, and frequency of the painting differ according to region, climate, sect, and society. Women in some areas decorate their homes only once each year, in preparation for the Divali Festival honoring Lakshmi. In other regions women paint the walls and floors of their houses for many religious occasions during the year. The paintings are associated with annual festivals for different deities and with the samskaras. For example, for Divali, women in western India prime their walls with a base coat of locally mined red ochre. Then, because the weather is too dry to grow rice, they use a pigment made from white lime to cover the walls with lace-like patterns of peacocks, tigers, elephants, and other animals. For each samskara held in this region, specifically prescribed concentric diagrams are applied to the ground in front of the home's entrance. These patterns are believed to prevent evil and ensure a beneficial outcome to ensuing rituals.

In southern India, each day of the year is an occasion to create a new painting on the ground outside the front door. Except when rain makes the process impossible, the women in millions of homes rise before dawn to paint these *kolams*. Using rice flour or ground white stone powder, they either mark out a grid of dots and then connect them into an intricate design, or they work entirely freehand. On festival days they use colored powders to fill in the patterns. Originally all the symbols depicted were intended to protect the home by honoring the Gods, keeping evil spirits away, and encouraging good spirits to enter the home. Today these well-educated women employ both sacred and mundane symbols in their designs, priding themselves on their creativity and on the variety of their artistic expression. The purpose of kolams has extended beyond simple household worship; they have become icons of feminine virtue, strength, and spirit.[6]

*paradox*

In cities, where more and more families live in small nuclear units and many contemporary women work outside the home, time restraints have encouraged some new ways of acknowledging and thanking household deities. Samskaras are still occasions for elaborate and detailed rituals, but daily pujas are less complex than those of earlier generations. The Gods and Goddesses are honored, but the prayers are shorter. The limited space in apartment buildings means that flowers and fruit must be purchased in the market, not grown in the garden. Tulasi is raised in a small pot on a windowsill. Many women have no time to paint decorations, although some in the south will still sketch out quick kolams in the halls in front of their doors or, if they can afford it, hire someone to paint more elaborate ones on the ground outside their buildings. Others purchase newly marketed gadgets that allow powdered designs to be rolled out in pre-set patterns. Some buy stick-on designs for their floors or walls. But even with all these contemporary adaptations to ancient customs, popular Hinduism is as vibrant as ever. Traditional values are blended with contemporary attitudes to create a new vitality and viability. For example, satellite television, initially decried for its negative influence, now carries numerous religious programs, which are as popular in India as soap operas are in the West. Like so many other developments in modern India, these innovative technologies reinforce spiritual perspectives. The home is still the center of activity and decisions in India, and the household shrine and rituals that surround it continue to be at the heart of the Hindu experience.

MUNIYANDIPURAM, THANJAVUR DISTRICT, TAMIL NADU

The women in more than a million households in this southern state create new sacred designs in front of their homes each day, as their ancestors did for centuries. The decorations last only an hour or two before being worn away underfoot.

89

*Honoring the Spirit*
*of Community*

FOUR

Although the light is less intense than earlier, the air is still hot and dusty. After spending the entire day at the back-breaking toil of picking cotton, Lalubhai and his wife, Meeraben, have just come home. They tiredly greet their four small children, the youngest still in the arms of his toothless grandmother. As they sip cups of milky tea and munch thick, sugary biscuits, they listen to the stories of the children's adventures while their parents were at work. Then it is time to get ready to go to the shrine.

Meeraben retires to the walled washroom to clean off the day's dust and to change into her brightest red sari, tie-dyed in yellow and green. She puts on her best jewelry: large silver anklets and bracelets, several rings, long earrings studded with semi-precious stones, and a thick silver necklace. Lalubhai bathes right in the courtyard, stripped down to his underwear, splashing water over himself and lathering profusely before rinsing clean. He wraps a *lungi* (sarong) around his waist and legs in order to discreetly change into clean *pajamas*, surmounted by a fresh *khadi kurta* (handspun cotton tunic). He then takes a five-yard length of fine cotton cloth dyed in a rainbow of bold colors and wraps it around and around his head to create an elegant turban. Two gold and zircon studs in his ears, a silver amulet around his neck, and his watch are his only jewelry. Lalubhai's mother had washed and dressed the children before their parents arrived home. Then, with the children's eight cousins, two uncles, and three aunts, the family is ready to leave the house. All are dressed in their finery, and the mood is one of gaiety and anticipation.

PRECEDING PAGES
NAGPUR, PURI DISTRICT, ORISSA

A farmer prostrates himself in prayer beneath a sacred *peepul* tree that his village worships as the Goddess-Spirit of their community.

OPPOSITE
HODKO, KACHCH DISTRICT, GUJARAT

Most homes in western India are built around courtyards in which much of the household activity takes place.

As they walk down the street through the village of similar tile-roofed mud houses, they are joined by members of other families. It is Friday, the most auspicious day on which to worship Mataji, the deity that *is* the community.

Her pujas may take place at any time during the day, and some families were at her shrine as early as sunrise. Lalubhai's family prefer to approach her in the evening, when their duties are done and they can devote their entire minds to her service.

On the outskirts of the village, in the fields beyond the last house, is an ancient *peepul* tree. Its main trunk is over nine feet in diameter, and its lateral roots have grown into smaller trunks; the entire tree has a radius of a medium-sized house. Between the gnarly roots of the central trunk is a huge standing stone covered with orange-red vermilion. These, the tree and the stone, are Mataji, the Goddess who protects the village and provides for its welfare. No one knows how long she has been worshipped in this spot—quite possibly for a thousand years or more, probably since the first people settled the village. No Brahmanas live in this community, only farmers like Lalubhai and his family, craftsmen, a few merchants, and some Harijans (those in such occupations as cleaning sewers and disposing of the dead). The village is poor and has no money to hire a full-time priest. Instead, various families volunteer to take care of the shrine, sweeping around the tree every morning and placing fresh flowers on the rocks at its base. One of the village elders serves as the *pujari* (one who facilitates the pujas) each Friday and at the annual festival of the Goddess.

AMBUA, DHAR DISTRICT, MADHYA PRADESH

The sinuous lateral roots of an ancient peepul tree wind around a large upright stone that has been daubed with vermilion to represent the Goddess. Beneath the tree are terracotta horses given as part of pujas in gratitude for the beneficence of the Goddess.

Lalubhai, as the family's oldest male, carries a flat basket filled with freshly made sticky sweets, a small mound of white sugar lumps, some flowers just picked from alongside the village reservoir, a few cubes of camphor, and sticks of incense. Meeraben holds a deeper basket of fluffy cotton straight from their field. In its center is a simply sculpted clay horse, a gift to the Goddess in gratitude for this year's bountiful harvest. Lalubhai hands all the offerings to the old pujari, who places the cotton in a growing pile to one side and the terracotta horse just to the right of the red stone. He puts some of the flowers on the horse and the rest among those that already surround the stone. He puts the incense and camphor into a large brass arati tray and the basket of sweets and sugar with others near the tree's roots.

Almost one hundred villagers have assembled as the sun begins to set. The pujari lights the incense and waves it in front of the stone and around the roots before pushing the sticks into a hole in the ground at their base. He then leads the group in prayers to the Goddess, beginning with songs praising her name: "Om Mata, Mataji, Om Mata, Mataji." This is followed by a prayer: "You are the True One, the Auspicious, the Beautiful, the Purest Form of all the Gods. You are our Mother [Mataji]: you have given us our lives; you are with us now; you give us our future. You are the Protector: you keep us safe. You destroy evil and you bring us health. We sing your names, we sing your praises. You are our Mother [Mataji]. We are your children."

MYSORE, KARNATAKA

A young girl gives offerings of flowers to the roots of a sacred tree associated with the worship of Nagas (cobras).

As they sing, Lalubhai and Meeraben concentrate on the magnificence of the Goddess, on the prosperity that they have received through her bounty: healthy children, a good, strong family, a large new harvest of cotton and with it the promise of enough to live on throughout the coming year. They focus their thoughts on their gratitude for their community and for the balance in their lives within it. In their prayers they experience a sense of oneness, a direct link to the Goddess and to the world around them: they have darshan with Mataji.

The day is darkening, and the old pujari lights several clay lamps filled with oil. He uses one of these lamps to ignite the camphor mounded on the arati tray, which he then holds up in front of the tree while several others strike the clappers of the bells that hang from the tree's branches.

The noise is almost deafening as all the devotees again sing out: "Om Mata, Mataji, Om Mata, Mataji…" Meeraben, Lalubhai, his mother, his brothers, and their wives usher their children up to the arati and all hold their hands above the cool flame before raising their fingers to their closed eyelids. The puja is complete. The newly blessed sweets are returned to the family members, who begin to eat them immediately. The cotton will be given to a local weaver to make into cloth to dress the roots of the sacred tree. The horse remains where it was placed, its spirit believed to be magically transformed into a real horse for the Goddess's use in the heavens. Gradually it will crumble and be replaced by others given to the Goddess in return for answered prayers.

JAMBUGHODA, VADODARA DISTRICT, GUJARAT

Villagers return home after worshipping at their community shrine.

Lalubhai and his family join their neighbors on their walk back along the shadow-enfolded road to the village. Someone begins to hum a popular film tune, and others join in. Soon the whole group is singing the familiar words, their feelings in harmony through having participated together in the weekly ritual for Mataji. In honoring the village Goddess they have also honored their community, their occupations, and themselves. They feel refreshed and complete, ready to go home for dinner and bed, but also ready to begin the next week of demanding activities.

ach Hindu community on the Indian subcontinent has its own *gramadevata*, the deity regarded as synonymous with the locality and everything within it. Just as the home is viewed as a composite of the spirits of all of its inhabitants and of the materials that went into its construction, so also is the community a blend of its physical, spiritual, and emotional components. Every house, every street, all of the shops, the craft studios, the barns, the farms, the trees and bushes, the wells, the reservoirs and streams, the inhabitants (people, animals, and insects), the spirits of those who have lived and died there, and even the activities, thoughts, and emotions of everyone living there—all are part of one great spirit identified as a deity, a gramadevata. This deity is the community, just as the community is the deity. They are inseparable.

Towns and cities have many individual subsections, each of which usually has its own gramadevata. For example, every small locality in the Rajasthan city of Jodhpur has a God or Goddess that has been worshipped in that spot for as long as the community has existed. While most cities are internally divided into numerous smaller entities, a municipality may also be viewed as one great deity, interwoven with all the inclusive gramadevatas. In this way, the entire southern Indian city of Madurai is believed to be the Goddess Meenakshi, the gramadevata of the initial community that lived there.[1] Her power is believed to be so immense that several kingdoms during the past millennia have owed their greatness to her beneficence. Many thousands of pilgrims from all over India visit her temple for her darshan every year.

Most gramadevatas are feminine—associated with the earth, fertility, healing, and protection. Their names often reflect their association with the Mother Goddess: they are usually prefixed or suffixed with *Ma*, *Mata*, *Matrika*, or *Amman* (each a regional translation of "mother"), *Ben* or *Bai* (sister), or *Rani* (queen). Sometimes their regional identities have been merged with that of a greater pan-Indian deity, such as Durga or Mari. For example, the gramadevata of many southern Indian communities is Mariamman, while seven temples to the Goddess DurgaMa surround and guard the royal city of Udaipur. According to Hindu numerology, seven is particularly auspicious. Seven Mothers (Saptamatrika) are believed to guard many towns throughout the subcontinent, each mother a specific aspect of the great Divine who may be beseeched in times of particular need. Together they are inseparable from the community that they incorporate. Their images may be delicately carved to delineate the various attributes of the individual Goddesses, but most often they are represented simply by a row of seven sacred stones placed beneath an ancient tree.[2]

PRECEDING PAGES

THIRUPARAN KUNDRAM, MADURAI DISTRICT, TAMIL NADU

Praying for fertility and successful childbirth, a young couple prostrate themselves on the platform of a community shrine in the center of a southern village.

OPPOSITE

ROOPAN DEVI DEVARA, UDAIPUR DISTRICT, RAJASTHAN

Sacred trees are as varied as the communities they represent. Beneath this ancient tree, a large wooden sculpture is carved with multiple images of the Goddess Roopan Devi and with animals associated with her protection.

Although gramadevatas are indivisible from their communities, each must have a focal point, a specific place or object on which to direct attention. The *devasthana*, or shrine, of a gramadevata is usually associated with an important natural feature: a hill, a boulder, a stream or pond, a tree or grove of trees. Trees are by far the most common: there are hundreds of thousands of sacred trees being worshipped constantly in India. Most are ancient, venerated as gramadevatas for untold centuries in the same way that the peepul tree is worshipped by Lalubhai and his family. The appearance of these tree sanctuaries is as varied as the communities themselves: sometimes there are several trees together, or a single tree with a large platform built around it, or one marked with flags and banners, or one with its trunk dressed like the Goddess herself. The devasthana may be in the center of the village or in the fields beyond the farthest house. When the tree dies, the spot remains sacred. It is believed to be vibrant with the energies of innumerable pujas and will usually continue to be a focus of community worship, most often with a platform or building constructed where the tree stood.[3]

CUMBUM, MADURAI DISTRICT, TAMIL NADU

Offerings tied in bits of cloth have been fastened to the lateral roots of this peepul tree as a part of prayers to the Goddess Durga. To the upper left is a string of small rolls of paper, each containing the names of the Goddess written in longhand 1,008 times as a gesture of honor.

The shrines in Brahmana villages or those with Brahmana occupants are usually overseen by Brahmana priests. Pujas that take place in devasthanas in those many communities without Brahmana occupants are often facilitated by non-Brahmana priests, often because the community simply may not be able to afford to hire a Brahmana. Conversely, a single Brahmana in a village might feel isolated and therefore not want to move there. The position of priest may be hereditary, usually given to a person of a menial caste whose family has conducted the pujas at a devasthana for untold generations. In some villages, however, inhabitants share responsibility for the shrine and appoint respected citizens to conduct worship, like the pujari in Mataji's shrine. Many rituals that take place in a devasthana are conducted by individual devotees without an intermediary. The contact is direct between devotee and deity.

Occasionally the spirit of community, the gramadevata, may be transformed into that of another, greater deity. For example, the essence of the tiny Orissan village of Padmapoda is viewed as the Goddess Gelubai, a local Thakurani, or benign form of the Divine Feminine honored within a sacred tree. Gelubai is believed to protect and nurture every aspect of existence within Padmapoda's boundaries. At times of great need, however, when an individual, a family, or the entire village requires the aid of Shakti (the dynamic power of the Great Goddess), then a special puja is enacted in which the identity of Gelubai is subsumed into that of the Goddess Chandi. Perhaps someone is particularly ill and is unable to be cured by doctors, or perhaps the village is suffering a drought that endangers its crops and livelihood. In these and other dire cases a special Brahmana priest will be hired to perform the puja.

Gelubai is first bathed, dressed, and adorned, as she is every day, and her usual puja is conducted. Next, an area is cleaned on the platform in front of the tree; a sacred diagram is drawn with special powders, and a fire is laid with sticks of wood. Then the flames are made to flare by being anointed with ghee, during which time the priest sings the names and attributes of the Goddess Chandi. As he extols her, he places a coconut in the flames and invites the Goddess to pour her divine energy into the tree, thereby transforming its essence from that of the village into the universal power of the Absolute. As the coconut heats, the milk within it boils, causing it to burst, which signals the moment when the transformation is complete. Chandi in all her strength is then present within the village. Her devotees may have direct darshan with her. They believe that whatever they pray for will happen and that by this ritual miracles do occur. The sick person will be healed or the drought ended. Once the puja is complete and the invocations made, Chandi is reverently thanked and invited to leave the site. The tree returns once more to Gelubai as the village returns to its peaceful farming existence.

PADMAPODA, PURI DISTRICT, ORISSA

Several centuries of daily applications of black oil and red vermilion to one spot on this sacred tree in a small village in eastern India has resulted in a raised lacquer mound that is treated as the face of the Goddess Gelubai. Bangles have been tied as offerings to the Goddess during prayers by women for the health of their families.

Although the majority of Indian communities worship feminine gramadevatas, many communities envision these deities as masculine. In some regions it is common to worship a local form of Rama or Hanuman as gramadevata. In these cases indigenous legends usually involve the deity's interaction with local sites and historical characters that are unique variations of the more common mythology. Many villages refer simply to their God as Baba or Appan (two words for father) or an appellation that incorporates one of these names. Just as Mataji is considered the mother of Lalubhai's village, in other communities deities are visualized as judicious and powerful fathers who protect their families from danger.

In the eastern part of the northern Indian state of Uttar Pradesh, many towns and villages have two gramadevatas—one masculine, the other feminine—each housed in its own tree shrine. The local names of these Gods and Goddesses are as varied as their communities, although the generic name for the God is either Baba or Di-Baba, while the Goddess is called Kali-Ma. Both are considered tutelary deities: they protect their devotees from adversity. Villagers may pray to either or both, depending on inclination and need. An outsider would have difficulty ascertaining the difference between the two tree shrines that honor the God and Goddess, except when terracotta offerings have been made. When devotees request the aid of Di-Baba, it is customary to promise to give him a terracotta horse when their prayers are answered. If a boon is received, the worshipper will commission this sculpture to be made by a local potter. On a day considered auspicious to the God, the horse will be placed in his devasthana, along with gifts of flowers and food.

Each day the image of Gelubai is bathed in holy water and daubed with fresh applications of oil and vermilion. Then a fresh sari is wrapped around the tree and pleated in front. Finally, jewelry is applied to her ears and forehead, and flowers are placed all around her.

Pujas to Kali-Ma are more popular than those to Di-Baba. Kali-Ma is viewed locally as the Mother Goddess and is petitioned for aid when any kind of problem strikes
the family. Her followers may come from any Hindu sect. Her pujas are considered
particularly effective in combating agricultural calamities, family crises, civic disputes,
infertility, and disease. Many believe her to be both the cause and the cure of smallpox, cholera, and measles. When struck with one of these diseases, a person is said to
be inhabited by Kali-Ma. Part of the cure is to worship and honor the Goddess within. Often the worshipper will promise that if the Goddess answers his or her prayers,
then terracotta elephants will be given to her. These elephants are
believed to become real animals in the spirit world the instant they
are placed in her shrine, and many believe that Kali-Ma rides them
in her nightly battles against evil. Once the elephants have been
given and transformed by the Goddess, they no longer have any
value. They, like the horses given to Di-Baba, remain beneath the
tree to disintegrate with the weather, their sole purpose fulfilled.[4]

Terracotta gifts are placed in the shrines of gramadevatas throughout
India. Most often made on commission by local potters, they are easily affordable, even in a country where the overall per capita income
is particularly low. Their form and the style of production vary
according to local tradition. Many are simple stick figures made of
dowels of clay, others are sculpted of elements thrown on the wheel,
while still others are made by coil or slab techniques, or mass-produced in molds. They range in size from just inches high to over
sixteen feet, the largest terracottas known in the history of mankind.
Almost all are gifts to local gramadevatas in grateful response to the
deities' beneficence. Each, even the most elaborate, is ephemeral: its
value is in the giving. It represents a personal commitment between
the devotee and his or her deity, the essence of Hindu reciprocity.[5]

Considering that each Hindu community honors its own individual
gramadevata, it is no wonder that India is said to contain a million
and one Gods and Goddesses. The present census lists more than 630,000 villages, not
counting the numerous towns and cities. In its entirety, the Hindu pantheon is overwhelming, inconceivable. Its relevance lies in its approachability, not its vastness. Each
Hindu has a vital sense of belonging. Each has an ishtadevata, the deity of personal
choice; a kuladevata, the deity of family and household; and a gramadevata, the deity
of community. An individual's life is entwined in recognizing and honoring these relationships, in defining the self and one's interconnectedness to all other living beings. In
a world where concepts and values are constantly challenged, the underlying purpose
of all the numerous rituals and pujas of every day and season is to allow the Hindu to
meet God, an experience that brings with it a sense of clarity, balance, and belonging.

PRECEDING PAGES
PADMAPODA, PURI DISTRICT,
ORISSA

In a rare ritual, a fire is built on a temporary sacred diagram in front of
Gelubai's tree. Two priests alternately
feed the fire with ghee while intoning
verses to the Supreme Goddess
Chandi (a form of Parvati), requesting
her divine presence in the village.

OPPOSITE
KUSHINAGAR, DEORIA DISTRICT,
UTTAR PRADESH

This small village shrine contains no
image of a deity. Instead, the simple
iron *trishula* (trident) and the cement
*pinda* (cone) represent the Goddess
Kali-Ma. The terracotta elephant, a
gift from a grateful devotee, is
believed to become a real mount for
the Goddess in the spirit world for
her nightly battles against evil.

# Answered Prayers:
# The Evolution from
# Shrine to Temple

FIVE

The entire city seems to be awake and on the move even though it is only 7 A.M. The streets are filled with activity and the cacophony of vendors and traffic. Vivek and Manika have finished their cups of coffee and are ready to go to the temple. Their marriage festivities were held just two weeks ago, and the new bride and bridegroom have been advised that it would be auspicious to visit several important sacred sites before they settle down. They have already traveled by bus to five other temples in central southern India; but today is the most important: in this town is an ancient temple dedicated to an image of Shiva renowned for his powers of granting fertility and successful childbirth.

Manika is reverentially dressed in her finest pink sari and gold jewelry, and Vivek wears a traditional white silk dhoti, his chest bare to expose the sacred thread that all Brahmana men wear. As they walk down the wide avenue that approaches the temple, they buy a basket of offerings from one of the stalls and then stop to wash their hands and feet in the waters of the ancient stone pool that stands just to the left of the temple compound. Leaving their sandals at one side, they pass through massive doors under a towering stone structure filled with niches containing sculptures of the Gods and mythological figures.

They immediately notice a change in atmosphere. It is not quiet here, but the intensity of noise is different. There are no vehicles, no market stalls, just throngs of people going in different directions and involved in many activities. They join the mass of people moving to the left in a wide walled passageway that encircles the central temple. As they walk, they compose their minds to focus on the reason that they are here: to pray for pregnancy and a

successful childbirth. Their attention is diverted by the many rooms built into the enormous stone wall at their left. Some contain the sculpted carts and animal-shaped litters for carrying the processional images of the deities; others hold offices for the temple administrators; some are the kitchens for cooking the food offered to the Gods; and still others are stalls for the temple elephant and for the cows that provide milk for the pujas. Everywhere there is activity. The elephant, its head colorfully painted with vines and lotuses, reaches out its trunk to bless passersby in return for offerings of coins. A group of women squat in a circle singing songs. Children run among the devotees playing a game of tag. Pilgrims are stretched out asleep between the carved columns of a roofed platform. The smell of spices wafts from a large group sitting together eating rice and lentils off plates made from large green banana leaves.

As Vivek and Manika turn a corner they come upon an ancient tree, its branches tied with bundles of cloth offerings and prayers written on bits of paper in a tiny flowing script. Beneath it are stone sculptures of cobras, some with human bodies: the Nagas, ancient Gods of healing and fertility. Manika opens a small tin she has been carrying in her purse and smears sandalwood paste on the sculptures, praying as she does so for the health of their firstborn child.

*what's the pt. of praying if your karma is pre-determined? for dharma?*

Finally, after walking almost a quarter-mile around the enclosure, Vivek and Manika return to their starting point and enter a second gate. Inside, although still crowded, the atmosphere is more intense, focused on prayer. Again they turn left along a corridor that encircles the central temple. They are progressively drawing closer, ritually preparing themselves for their encounter with the great God. The edge of this passageway is

MYLAPORE, CHENNAI (MADRAS), TAMIL NADU

Families often gather in the temple to participate in complex personal rituals that involve the preparation of foods and the drawing of sacred diagrams. Some of the ceremonies require the participation of priests, but many are conducted by family members themselves, often just the women, who reenact prescribed rites that have been passed from mother to daughter for centuries.

SRI RANGAM, TIRUCHIRAPPALLI, TAMIL NADU

Many temples have their own resident elephants that, among other activities, place their trunks lightly upon the heads of devotees as an act of blessing.

119

arrayed with a series of small shrines, some with images of Shiva, many dedicated to Gods and Goddesses secondary to his worship, and others to Shiva's saints. Although the young couple are intent on their goal of puja to the central image of Shiva, they still stop to acknowledge each shrine as they pass, folding their hands in respect and touching them to their foreheads.

At last they enter the third and final gate. Directly in front of them is a huge plinth, on which sits a gigantic granite sculpture of the bull Nandi, the beloved mount of the Lord Shiva. He faces away from them and directly toward the open door of the main temple. This interior building is a large edifice, its exterior walls inlaid with numerous niches, each holding an image of a God or Goddess, crowned by an elaborate tower rising in sculpted tiers to resemble the peak of a fantastic mountain. Vivek and Manika are overcome with awe. As they walk around this building, they, like the rest of the crowd, are quiet, concentrating on their prayers. When the newlyweds return to Nandi's shrine they begin to climb the steps into the temple's entrance hall. Inside it is cool, the light filtered from windows on each side. Both the pillars and the ceiling they support are elaborately carved with images of Shiva, his wife, Parvati, and their sons, Ganesha and Kartikeya, along with many other Gods, demigods, and mythical beings.

Ahead of them is the sanctum sanctorum, the heart and soul of the entire temple complex. The crowd pushes them tightly together and, so that their offerings are not spilled, they hold them high above their heads as they join the line to enter the inner shrine. As they pass over the threshold into this final room, a Brahmana priest takes their offerings and asks their names, their community, and the stars under which they were born. Inside, the walls are plain and very dark, encrusted with centuries of smoke from countless lamps. The strong smell of incense and congested air permeates

everything. The noise of chanting and bells fills their ears. There is a sense of oneness with the rest of the crowd of devotees as they all press forward, straining to see into the dark recess of the small central chamber. Several priests are inside. One holds a lighted lamp and circles it around and around the stone image of the God Shiva. It is a Linga, a pillar shape that for Hindus represents this supreme deity. This Linga is swyambhu, not carved by any hand of man but believed to be naturally formed by the God himself. It has been worshipped here for thousands of years, long before the temple was built. Shiva's devotees believe that this Linga is radiant with power, vibrant with the ability to grant any wish. A second Brahmana priest rings a bell while a third, the one who had taken the offerings from Vivek, places his basket and others at the Linga's base and then proceeds to chant prayers to the God, reciting the names, communities, and stars of each of the devotees. Manika and Vivek feel thrilled by their sense of Shiva's presence and magnificence. Silently they ask him to give them a healthy child; they feel sure that their prayers will be answered. One priest brings out the arati, and they put their hands into the flame and put white ash on their foreheads. The other priest returns to them their basket of prashad. Then they are pushed by the crowd out a side door and into the courtyard next to the temple. Feeling blessed, they silently return straight through each of the gates and out onto the still-busy street. These newlyweds believe that their lives have just been changed. They have passed through the many stages of preparation to meet their God. They have made their prayers, had Shiva's darshan, and received his blessing. Now they can take the long train ride back to their home to begin their new lives together, content in the knowledge that they will create a new generation to carry on their family traditions.

KOTILINGESHWARA, KOLAR DISTRICT, KARNATAKA

The most sacred image in any temple to Shiva is the Linga, an aniconic pillar resting in a base and symbolizing the union of opposites. Many Shiva temples have a central Linga in primary worship along with many subsidiary ones that were given by devotees throughout history. This temple boasts the most: 8.5 million Lingas!

Each temple in India is different: its architecture, decoration, size, and contents are unique to its own history and purpose. Most are built on sites that have been in worship for as long as anyone knows. The central image in many is primordial—a natural stone that has been viewed as a God or Goddess for millennia, like the Swyambhu Linga in the temple just described. The structures around these images have been built over the centuries through the contributions of grateful devotees.

A temple's growth is entirely based on the Hindu concept of reciprocity, as discussed in Chapter 2. In contacting a God or Goddess in puja, a devotee's desires may be implicit, without a special request, or may include prayers for something specific, such as good employment or increased wealth or improved health. In either case devotees who consequently experience good luck must share their fortune in acts of kindness and also in honoring the deity to whom they have prayed. A greater fortune demands a bigger repayment. A large temple may well have begun as a shrine to a local gramadevata.

Today many temples are being built on the spots where gramadevatas have been worshipped for centuries. When a positive change happens in the village, gifts are given to the local tree shrine. In contemporary India, the economy of the burgeoning middle class is improving rapidly. Many people have relatives who send them money from overseas; new technologies at home have created new jobs; better education engenders more employment choices. Whatever the source of improvement, the recipient must thank his or her deities with presents. Often the community will join together to give something to the shrine; they may raise money through subscription, or particularly fortunate individuals may make large donations on their own. Accordingly, a family may give money to the local shrine to erect a new platform or even a small building. Another family may commission a stone sculpture of the God or Goddess to be carved and placed in the shrine. Someone else may want his own ishtadevata to be honored by financing the building of a secondary shrine. The accoutrements of puja may be improved: large bells may be tied to the tree, fine arati plates and lamps given, and jewelry commissioned to adorn the sacred stones or the new images. Gradually the wealth of the shrine grows, and locking doors must be installed to protect the new objects from theft. The consequence of all this change is that the atmosphere in the shrine changes.

Decisions must then be made regarding the care of the larger complex. Are there funds to employ a caretaker? Should the pujas continue to be conducted by non-Brahmana pujaris, or should a Brahmana priest be hired? The answers to these questions may well alter the dynamics of the shrine. Many non-Brahmana communities that have for centuries conducted their pujas according to their own traditions choose to change with the times, to modernize by employing Brahmanas. The reasons are complex: Brahmana priests have been trained since childhood in the intricate prescriptions of rituals, underlining the implicit message that the pujas they conduct are more pleasing to the Gods than those of non-Brahmanas; and broad social pressure suggests that Brahmana superiority will improve the status of the community.[1] (Brahmana priests are always male, organized in large temples into complex hierarchies. Occasionally pujaris in non-Brahmana shrines and temples are female, further complicating the choice.) Not all enlarging shrines choose to hire Brahmana priests. Some continue to retain the services of their traditional pujaris. But usually the rituals conducted by these non-Brahmana priests are amended to fit the stature of the changed surroundings.

CUMBUM, MADURAI DISTRICT, TAMIL NADU

Both photographs on this page show the same sacred tree shrine dedicated to the Goddess Durga. In just five years the number of images and decorations under the tree has grown extensively (the small white wall in the center of the top picture is the same as the one shown in the lower right of the bottom picture). All have been given as grateful acknowledgments of answered prayers. The rapid expansion suggests the probability that a temple will be built on this spot before long.

If the good fortune of individuals or the entire community continues to increase, then architects and stone carvers may be hired to build a complete temple. The style of the temple is usually governed by that of the local architecture, although recent growth in the influence of mass media and the popularity of certain historical and contemporary styles have resulted in new, eclectic Hindu temple architecture in India and abroad. (Many new Hindu temples are already in use in North America and Europe, and others are continually being built.)[2] Nevertheless, this trend simply continues a historical precedent: temples have always grown through the combined influences of reciprocal donations, traditional values, and fashionable technology. The architecture of many of India's most important ancient temples is an eclectic blend of many regional styles.

Virtually all of India's temples have grown through this process: either gradually, through the donations of grateful individuals and groups, or rapidly, through the sponsorship of one powerful and wealthy person. Many of the most magnificent temples were built by royalty. For example, a king might create an enormous stone edifice for two purposes: to demonstrate gratitude to his God for his position and to proclaim to his subjects his supreme sovereignty.[3] Some of the finest temples recently constructed in India, including the Birla Temple in Calcutta, were financed by the country's new rich.

A new temple most often stands directly on a spot that has been a focus of worship for generations. In some cases a building will be constructed to incorporate a sacred tree. More often the requirements of a large building will mean that the new central shrine is situated alongside or even some distance from the tree.

Special rituals are carefully enacted to cleanse and purify the new area before construction begins. The architecture of the new building will be carefully planned so that its proportions and alignment both cater to the demands of ritual and facilitate the needs of worship. Decisions must be made as to whether to continue using the natural stones or sculpted images that have been the focus of pujas or to carve or cast new sculptures. The form of a new image may portray the iconography of a pan-Indian God or Goddess or may accentuate the personality of the local deity. If the ancient image is to be installed in the new temple, then special ceremonies are enacted to ensure its proper transference to the new sanctum. The Swyambhu Linga worshipped by Vivek and Manika was originally established in this manner when the Shiva temple was built many centuries ago. Even after the primary images are transferred from an older sacred site to a new temple, unofficial pujas generally continue at the original spot. Sacred trees, like the Naga tree, remain in worship inside temple compounds throughout India.

If a new image is to be consecrated, then elaborately prescribed rituals must be followed precisely to transfer the energy of the deity from its original source. The final act in the consecration of any new image, whether in household, shrine, or temple, is the ritual opening of the eyes, which facilitates darshan, enabling the deity to see as well as be seen. At the last moment, eyes may be chiseled in or painted on or added in metal or stone before the life force is breathed into the image (*prana pratishtha*), bringing it full divine consciousness. Now the deity is believed to be fully present in the image, allowing it to be bathed, dressed, adorned, and honored in the manner befitting a God or Goddess.

HOSPET, BELLARY DISTRICT, KARNATAKA

Temple architecture has always been a reflection of contemporary values and styles. This shrine, built by a grieving widower in honor of his wife, combines traditional prototypes with fantasy themes suggested by popular cinema and poster art.

Occasionally a temple will be built on an entirely new spot. Over the past two centuries, as the Indian population has increased by a thousand percent, many undeveloped areas have been settled. Industrialization created new factory towns, and increased commerce and changes in government engendered new cities and suburbs. All of these communities require shrines, and many have sponsored the construction of temples. The process of selecting the site for a temple is complicated. Astrologers and seers are consulted, and the history and legends of the property assessed. There should be no demons or ghosts associated with the site, and any negativity must be removed through complex purification rituals. If possible, the temple should be near water, preferably a pond, river, or stream. If not, then water must be accessible either by well or reservoir. A temple is usually aligned on an east-west axis so that the entrance and all of the subsidiary gates, where applicable, are directly in front of the inner sanctum. Ancient scriptures govern the ground plan of the temple and the position of all the subsidiary buildings to conform to the delineations of a sacred geometric diagram, or *mandala*.

This large square mandala is divided into a grid of many smaller squares, each associated with positions of the stars, sun, moon, and planets, and with the deities related to these heavenly bodies. The sanctum is placed at the center of the mandala—all other buildings, walls, and entrance ways revolve around it. The temple compound is thus a microcosm, a conscious replica of the conceptual universe. It functions not only as a seat of the Gods but also as a metaphysical means of transcending the exterior worlds and entering the center, visualized as the matrix of creation. Consequently, the entire temple plan is intended to assist the progression of the devotee from mundane existence to divine realization.[4]

## GARBA GRHA

The inner sanctum of the temple is called the *garba grha*, literally translated as "chamber of the womb." It holds within its dark and unadorned recesses the potency of the central image, the Absolute Power of the God or Goddess. No one but qualified priests is allowed to enter here—to do so might adulterate the purity of the power. Even the priests must undergo rituals of purification each time they wish to enter this "womb." All other devotees approach as close to the image as possible for darshan with the deity. In some temples they are allowed to touch the base of the image or the feet of the Divine, believing that by doing so they absorb the God's radiance through their fingertips. Non-Hindus are not permitted to enter the innermost areas of many of the most important temples, as it is feared that by inappropriate thoughts or gestures they might desecrate the image.[5] Some temples, such as the Jagannath Temple in Puri, are considered so pure that no non-Hindus may enter the compound at all.

The path to the inner sanctum is intentionally long in order to properly prepare the devotee for an encounter with the deity. The process is achieved through *pradakshina* (ritual circumambulation), in which the individual walks around the center several times, symbolically shedding more of the mundane world with each pass. In large compounds this is achieved through a series of up to five concentric corridors—the nearer to the central temple, the more sacred the corridor. The final pradakshina is made in a windowless passage that surrounds the chamber of the womb. All existence is focused on the sacred. All five senses are then activated as the devotee reaches the inner sanctum: bells ring and priests chant; lamps and arati are lighted; incense and ghee burn; the heat of the fire is felt with one's fingers; and prashad is eaten. For the devout, a sixth sense is also activated: the sense of the presence of the Divine.

The position of the womb chamber within the temple is usually marked by a tower or dome, its fluidity of line and refined decoration contrasting directly with the dark simplicity of the inner chamber. Hinduism, in common with many other religions, associates mountain peaks with sacred purity and deems them the abode of the Gods. Shiva and his wife, Parvati, are believed to live on Mount Kailasa in the Himalayas. Many Hindu saints have achieved enlightenment in these mountains, and a pilgrimage trek around the sacred peaks is believed to bring great spiritual merit. The towers of many temples are built to resemble stylized mountains reminiscent of these peaks. Many are elaborately carved in stages from ground to spire, some beginning with animals and the mundane activities of man on the lower levels, sacred symbols and celestial figures at the middle range, and Gods and Goddesses at the top. The capstone or flag on the peak is directly above the primary image, accentuating, by its height and by the progressive arrangement of its levels, the same process of sacred transformation.[6]

KHAJURAHO, CHATARPUR DISTRICT, MADHYA PRADESH

Through a combination of destruction and neglect, many of northern India's ancient temples no longer exist. An exception, this eleventh-century temple exemplifies the classical style of the region: its central pinnacle, built directly over the primary image of the God Shiva, is intended to resemble the cosmic mountain, abode of the Gods at the center of the universe.

Styles of temple architecture vary greatly throughout the subcontinent, and the contrast is particularly pronounced between the north and south. The tower, or *shikhara*, above a northern Indian temple is usually tall, its verticality continuing the niches and tiers of the projecting walls in a fluid line from base to peak. The *vimana*, or building holding the womb chamber, in a southern Indian temple is generally a flatter structure with a proportionately smaller pyramidal tower to represent the cosmic mountain. The entrance gates are enormous, elaborately sculpted structures with barrel-vaulted caps; they are visible from great distances to entice the devotee to prayer. In contrast, northern Indian temple gateways are usually relatively understated, their shikharas drawing the devotee's attention.

The differences between north and south are further underlined by a comparison of the numbers of remaining ancient temples. Islam spread into India in the eighth century, and over the next eleven centuries countless Hindu temples were either destroyed in the name of Allah or allowed to fall into disuse and decay through lack of patronage, particularly in the north, where Muslim influence had its strongest impact. Few ancient temple complexes remain there. Urban temples were forced into smaller spaces, often moving into buildings with businesses and into living quarters; while small rural temples either were unthreatened or were torn down and rebuilt later. The exceptions were among isolated kingdoms in the central plateau and on the east coast, and those of powerful maharajahs in western India who made political and economic liaisons with Muslim rulers. Consequently, the contemporary northern states of Orissa, Madhya Pradesh, Rajasthan, and Gujarat retain many magnificent temples. In contrast, most southern Indian temples were protected from wide-spread destruction by Muslim invaders because of their geographic boundaries and the consolidated strength of strong Hindu kingdoms. The greatest number and largest of India's temple complexes are in the south, and many have grown steadily throughout history. For example, the huge temple to Vishnu in Sri Ranganatha, first constructed in the tenth century, has been expanded and changed in every century since then. The sculpted superstructure of its seventh outer gateway was just completed in 1987.

## SHIVA

Although Shiva is worshipped throughout India, the south is particularly famous for its temples to this God. For many he is the supreme deity, whose unimaginable power manifests on earth when and where he is needed. He is described in many ways: the Lord of Music; the King of Dance, whose movements are the energy that drives the universe; an absolute ascetic, whose purity keeps all existence in balance; the Creator and the Destroyer, who maintains the cycles of life and death; the Protector, who wards off evil; the greatest of all teachers, who explains the meaning of life to Gods and holy men; and the dedicated husband, whose deep love and passion for Parvati is a prototype of marital fidelity. To the Hindu, Shiva is unimaginable without Parvati. His form as Ardhanari (described in Chapter 1) portrays that she is half of his existence, in absolute equilibrium (his right half masculine, his left half feminine).[7]

BIKANER, RAJASTHAN

One priest pours holy water over a Shiva Linga while another recites sacred verses to the God. This black marble image is carved with four faces, each depicting a specific aspect of the Divine.

VARANASI, UTTAR PRADESH

A large copper Linga and Yoni stand on a tall plinth facing the cremation grounds on the banks of the sacred Ganges River. Their presence protects the sanctity of this space and is intended to provide guidance to the departing spirit.

Although Shiva may be worshipped for all the attributes listed above, his principal image in temples is aniconic: its form is symbolic rather than representational. The shape of the Linga is generally a column rounded at the top and resting in a *Yoni* (a grooved, tray-shaped base). Many references describe the Linga's phallic nature—the Linga (masculine) resting in the Yoni (feminine)—but this description is offensive to most Hindus. They state that the earliest Lingas are swyambhu (natural forms created by God, not by mankind), like the image worshipped by Manika and Vivek; and that those historical Lingas that were sculpted to resemble phalluses are stylistic aberrations. For them, the Linga is the primordial shape of God, and descriptions of its sexual symbolism demean and delimit his divine universality. Whatever the belief, Hindus view the consecrated Linga as the manifestation of Shiva's supreme power in every area of existence. It signifies the union of opposites in pure balance: creation and destruction, life and death, light and dark, good and evil. A Linga is the focus of each womb

chamber in all temples to Shiva, honored with the same reverential ministrations as the primary images in all other Hindu temples. It is God on earth, resplendent in all his magnificence.[8]

The shape of the Linga in most temples and shrines is simple, its smooth surfaces unembellished with carving. Some Lingas, however, are sculpted with the God's *mukha* (humanlike face). Some Mukha Lingas have only one face, while others are carved with four faces that depict Shiva's principal characters: fearsome, benign, ascetic, and sensuous. For example, the primary image of worship in the Sri Laleshwar Mahadev Temple in Bikaner, Rajasthan, is a black marble Chatur Mukha (four-faced) Linga. As the temple Brahmanas wash this Linga and adorn it during the preparatory rituals each day, they address each of these four integral images in order to acknowledge and activate that aspect of the Divine within their community. In some temples and household shrines in western India, particularly in the southwestern states of Maharashtra and Karnataka, the unadorned surface of a consecrated Linga is covered with a brass or silver mask on which a face of the deity and his associated symbols have been sculpted. Devotees believe that once the energy of the God has been invoked into the Linga, the raw power of the awakened image may be too strong for mortals and must be shielded. The mask serves that function. It will be placed on the Linga after bathing and before viewing by the public, to be removed only at night, when the image is "allowed to sleep."[9]

KOTILINGESHWARA, KOLAR DISTRICT, KARNATAKA

Before the plain granite Linga within this sanctum may be viewed by devotees, it is bathed and then covered by a large brass mask, surmounted by a hood of cobras (Nagas), and garlanded with flowers. The strength of the unadulterated image is considered to be so magnificent that without this shield it might render a common person senseless.

One of the major Hindu sects in southwestern India is called Lingayat, or Vira Shaiva. Lingayats worship Shiva as described through the teachings of a medieval saint, Basavanna, and carry a Linga with them at all times, usually hung from the neck or on the left arm. For many of Shiva's devotees the Linga represents sexual continence as well as fertility. The power of Shiva, and of his yogic ascetics, is believed to be enhanced through abstinence from sex. This withheld energy is thought to be transformed within the body into purity of soul. In this state, sacred energy is believed to ascend from the base of the spine to the crown of the head, irradiating in cosmic light.

One of the most magnificent temples to Shiva is called Brihadeshwara; it stands in the royal city of Thanjavur in the southern state of Tamil Nadu. When it was built a thousand years ago (finished in A.D. 1010), it was one of the tallest structures on earth. Its enormous compound is approached through two large gateways, the first with five sculpted tiers and the second with three. The inner courtyard is immense, divided into two large, equal squares. In the exact center of the first is an open-walled shrine to Nandi, Shiva's mount, symbolic of strength, faith, and constancy in belief. Carved entirely from one massive

granite boulder, Nandi stands level with and facing the Linga in the inner sanctum of the main sanctuary. The garba grha is situated in the center of the rear square. Rising 216 feet directly above it is a thirteen-tiered vimana, the height of a twenty-one-story building, surmounted by a single capstone weighing over eighty tons. The walls of the vimana are covered with niches holding impressive sculptures of Shiva. Surrounding the courtyard is a two-story pillared cloister containing shrines for 108 Lingas and numerous images of saints. The entire edifice was clearly designed to impress the devotee with the phenomenal power of both the God and the emperor who commissioned the temple.[10]

Pujas made at any time to the Linga at the Brihadeshwara Temple are considered auspicious, and the temple is always filled with pilgrims from all over India. Shiva's power is considered particularly potent during his festival, Mahashivaratri, held in the Hindu month of February–March, the most important time of the year to visit his temples. Close to a hundred thousand devotees converge on Brihadeshwara on this day to observe an all-night vigil of fasting, meditation, and prayer. Swarms push their way up the wide steps and into the two pillared halls that stretch one after the other toward the inner sanctum. A devotee determined to approach the enormous Linga must weave through a narrow passageway past several thousand men, women, and children sitting on the floor and chanting shlokas to Shiva. In the womb chamber many Brahmana priests stand on platforms to pour offerings of rosewater, coconut water, milk, yoghurt, five fruits, and sandalwood paste over a solid stone Linga twelve feet high and twenty-one feet in circumference. Hundreds of bronze lamps, refueled constantly with ghee, illuminate the sanctum. The tall chamber vibrates with the sounds of chanting priests and worshippers and the ringing of bells. Darshan with the Linga is described by Shiva's devotees as overpowering—the sense of his spirit is dazzling and stunning. After the long night's vigil they go home rejuvenated, attuned to the power of the God and to their responsibilities as conscientious Hindus, ready to begin another year.

## DEVI

Although Shiva is the primary power in the city of Thanjavur, his consort, Parvati, locally named Meenakshi, is the indisputable ruler of the neighboring royal city of Madurai. The sanctum of Shiva (known here as Sundareshwara, the "Beautiful One") is in the exact center of the city; Meenakshi's sanctum, right beside it, is the most popular. It is to her that devotees are advised to make their

most important pujas. In the sixteenth century the entire city was laid out as a cosmic mandala, with the enormous Meenakshi Sundareshwara Temple complex at its midpoint. Four wide rectangles of streets concentrically surround four sets of compound walls around the two interior temples. Four *gopuram* (gigantic gateways) mark the outer wall, the largest of which is sixty-six yards high. Each gopuram is covered with many hundreds of large, brightly polychromed sculptures of Gods, demons, guardians, and animals. Inside, every part of the compound is profusely sculpted (the official count, although not necessarily accurate, is 33 million sculptures). The entire complex is not only the physical center of the city, it is also the center of urban activity. At any given time of the day, and often late at night, there are thousands of people there. Countless smaller shrines vie with interior markets, selling everything from the accoutrements of puja to plastic toys and kitchen utensils. Tailors work alongside priests; crowds of pilgrims mix in with groups of schoolchildren; devotees eat and sleep right next to groups of women drawing sacred diagrams on the floor as part of prayers for successful marriages.[11]

MADURAI, TAMIL NADU

Central to the Meenakshi temple is this stepped reservoir in which devotees bathe before proceeding to the sanctums of the Goddess Meenakshi and her consort, Shiva. The betrothal and marriage of these deities are reenacted by millions of Hindus every year during twelve days of parades and festivities.

In the midst of all this confusion, devotees are advised to enter Meenakshi's gate first, bathe in the huge stepped pool that stands outside her temple, and then enter the inner gate to circumambulate her sanctum. Inside, her black stone image is adorned with some of India's most precious jewelry, its value incalculable; she has a different set for every day of the week and special sets for festival days.[12] Darshan with Meenakshi is said to be deeply enlightening, clearing a path from the brain to the heart.

Meenakshi is the patron deity, the gramadevata, of Madurai, her worship here probably antedating even the age-old worship of Shiva. She is envisioned as the bride of Shiva (Sundareshwara); but unlike brides in many other parts of India, Meenakshi is not submissive. She is a powerful, all-conquering warrior, and although legend portrays her as finally acquiescing to Shiva's might, in practice she is still considered the preeminent ruler. In her twelve-day festival each year in the Hindu month of April–May, the legends are reenacted of Meenakshi conquering all the male Gods and being crowned Queen of Madurai, the whole culminating in her marriage to Sundareshwara, in which she is unquestionably the dominant power. (Local lore refers to a female-dominated marriage as a Meenakshi relationship.) Over half a million devotees attend this festival. Each is reconfirmed as a loyal subject of the Goddess, unified into a spiritual kingdom through her supreme divine monarchy. In Madurai, the Goddess and her temple are ultimate, and all others, even her husband, are in her service.[13]

The principal deity of many Hindus throughout India is viewed as feminine, embodied as the Goddess known generically as Devi. Her individual names and identities are countless. As Mata, Ma, or Amma, she is the Cosmic Mother, the Womb of the Universe, from which all is born. As Bhagavati, she is the supreme deity governing all existence. As Shakti, she is pure dynamic power. Householders worship the Goddess Lakshmi for the health and welfare of their families. This Goddess of Abundance and Prosperity is also regularly worshipped by businessmen to ensure the success of their endeavors. For many the most important Goddess is Durga, the warrior deity who fights evil. She is prayed to for strength and clarity of purpose. Any of these Goddesses may be worshipped alone as a devotee's primary focus.

A Goddess may also be viewed as the consort or feminine complement of a major male deity. Parvati, as we have seen, is the Goddess consort of Shiva, integral to his worship. Radha is the consort of Krishna, a principal incarnation, or avatar, of the God Vishnu. Sita, the Goddess wife of Rama, another avatar of Vishnu, is the standard symbol of feminine virtue for most Hindus.

Gender does not appear to affect the personal choice of the devotee—both men and women worship the Divine Feminine. Within any given family it is just as likely that a man's ishtadevata will be a Goddess as a God. The same equality of choice is available to his wife and to their children.

Archaeological research suggests that the Goddess was widely worshipped in prehistoric India. Numerous invasions over the past thousands of years have brought with them male Gods and patriarchal systems. These early invaders did not, however, destroy the relative esteem for the feminine that had existed in India for thousands of years. The Indian subcontinent absorbed these invaders and their cultures as it has absorbed countless other invaders since that time. Hinduism is an intricate blend of all these influences. Western scholarship in India during the past two centuries has focused on the primary religious sects of the male deities Shiva and Vishnu. In doing so, it has largely ignored the massive coexisting worship of the Goddess. Today hundreds of millions of Hindus conduct regular pujas to the Goddess in one form or another. Although shrines to the Goddess are found everywhere in India (within larger temples, on roadsides, and in homes), there are fewer major temples devoted primarily to her. Nevertheless, her worship is vital and pervasive.[14]

In Hinduism, a religion of diversity, there are always exceptions to any rule. The southeastern state of Tamil Nadu contains many temples dedicated solely to Mariamman, a Goddess prayed to for her strength and protection (see the story that begins Chapter 2). For example, in the dark interior of her temple

PUNALUR, THANJAVUR DISTRICT, TAMIL NADU

The image of the Goddess Kali (known here as Bhagavati) in her form of raging power is often difficult for non-Hindus to understand. However, her devotees consider her protective and nurturing. No mother would willingly place her newborn child in front of anything that she found threatening. This baby has been brought here to instill her with the Goddess's strength. The mural depicts the Goddess disemboweling evil in the guise of beauty.

Worship of the Divine Feminine is primary to Hinduism. Temples and shrines to the Goddess are popular throughout India. She may be worshipped alone or as complemented by the Divine Masculine, most often viewed as her husband. Her forms are myriad; shown here are three aspects of the Goddess Parvati, two in her form as Durga.

in Samayapuram, Mariamman is depicted as a beautiful young woman smiling benignly while seated on a throne. Her eight hands hold the symbols of her power—of war and peace, of sanctity and severity—and under her right foot are the severed heads of three conquered demons. This temple and all her others throughout the state are always filled with devotees. Although some are men, most are women who pray to Mariamman for a variety of reasons: for good fortune in marriage, for health for their newborn children, for curing infertility, and for healing from disease. She is well known for granting wishes, and many miracles occur in her temples.

Bengal, in India's northeast, also contains many temples dedicated to the Goddess. Her most popular form is Kali, the ferocious feminine who re-creates life through destroying it. To the outsider, Kali is perhaps Hinduism's most confusing deity. She is often envisioned as a hideous black crone with pendulous breasts and lolling tongue, her neck adorned with a string of human skulls, her many hands brandishing weapons (one holding the bloody head of a demon), while she dances upon the seemingly lifeless form of Shiva. Kali is Shiva's wife in her most horrific form. According to legend, she has assumed her terrifying role to annihilate evil in all of its guises, but in her rage she devours all existence, even trampling the body of her husband, in order to re-create life. She symbolizes the absolute power of the Divine Feminine (Shakti) for action and change. For her devotees she is uncompromising and direct, demanding total surrender of the ego and detachment from materialism. She is intolerant of complacence and vanity, requiring from her followers rigorous self-honesty. But to her millions of devotees Kali is also the Divine Mother, the nurturer, the provider. To them, she is beautiful and beloved, enriching and fulfilling the lives of those who follow her path.

One of her most important temples is Kalighat, on the banks of the Ganges River in the heart of Calcutta (in fact, the city's name is an English corruption of the temple's name). The nineteenth-century buildings are white-plastered brick unadorned with sculptural decoration. Outside the compound's gates are hundreds of stalls selling prints and sculptures of the Goddess, along with the paraphernalia for household worship. Inside, the complex is always thronged with devotees, thousands lining up for darshan with Kali's swyambhu image (a natural blackened rock worshipped there since before the city was built). Each morning before the doors to her womb chamber are opened to her adoring public, the stone is washed with sacred substances. Then red eyes and a projecting golden tongue are affixed to her surface before she is crowned, dressed in red silk, and garlanded with flowers. Most of her devotees bring her offerings of flowers and fruit; but on important occasions, when her direct and powerful action is required to effect particular changes (for example, to heal an advanced case of cancer or to solve a vicious family dispute), Kali is offered the blood of freshly sacrificed goats. Robust, long-haired black rams are considered the most auspicious sacrifice, and worshippers bring them to Kalighat from all over the state. First the goat is worshipped, its spirit honored by putting vermilion and flowers on its head. Outside the temple, but within the compound, is a walled area containing a forked wooden stake. By burning incense and chanting mantras, a priest ritually purifies the stake and the surrounding area. The goat's neck is then placed in the forked stake while a non-Brahmana temple officiate prays over a large sword. In one movement he lifts the sword and quickly severs the head, catching it in a silver basin. At this moment all the assembled women ululate in high-pitched voices as the men shout, "Jai Kali! Jai Kali!" ("Kali Lives! Kali Lives!"). The head is then carried into the inner sanctum to be proffered to the image of the Goddess. Then it is brought out to be cooked with the rest of the goat and eaten as prashad by Kali's participating devotees.[15]

CALCUTTA, WEST BENGAL

The most important deity to many Hindus living in eastern India is the Goddess Kali. This central image in her famous temple of Kalighat is an uncarved black stone that has been worshipped in this spot for centuries. Slaughtered goats are offered to her by devotees who wish to show particular reverence.

## VISHNU

In contrast, Vishnu represents stability, order, and the maintenance of tradition. He is the God of Family Values, of Relationships and Equanimity. Known as the Preserver, it is he who maintains the balance of creation when it is threatened by demons or by one of the other Gods or Goddesses. His followers form one of the three main sects of Hinduism (the devotees of Shiva and Devi are the other two). One of the main features of the doctrines of Vishnu is the reciprocity of love: love between husband and wife, and love between deity and devotee. This love is exemplified through his relationship with his consort, Lakshmi, the Goddess of Abundance and Prosperity. Vishnu is viewed as a savior who has been reborn on earth many times to conquer and balance evil. In each incarnation Vishnu is accompanied by Lakshmi—proving the everlasting power of marital love.[16]

Of the ten avatars of Vishnu, the two most popular forms are Rama and Krishna. Each has its own specific cults with associated mythology, traditions, and rituals. Rama, the princely hero of the epic *Ramayana*, epitomizes loyalty, bravery, strength, and responsibility. His wife, Sita, is the traditional ideal Hindu woman: feminine, faithful, resilient, and pure. In the *Ramayana*, Rama and Sita are aided in their difficulties by the Monkey God, Hanuman. Worshipped in his own right, Hanuman is the symbol of unquestioning allegiance and dedication of purpose. There are temples and shrines to Rama throughout India. He is often portrayed as a hunter or warrior, holding his bow and arrows and attended by Sita, his loyal brother Lakshmana, and Hanuman. The name Rama is so revered that in many parts of India, particularly in the west, the word is synonymous with *God* and is used as a salutation between people.

Krishna is worshipped by more Hindus than any other of Vishnu's incarnations. Like Rama, he was born human, and the stories of his childhood and adolescence exemplify his mischievous character. Later, as the wise hero of the epic *Mahabharata*, he established the fundamental principles of practical Hinduism. He is passionate, valorous, just, thoughtful, and empathetic. Although his legends recount his many youthful amorous encounters, his subsequent marriage to Rukmini (Lakshmi) is, like that of Rama and Sita, the prototype for Hindu marriage. In his shrines he is often depicted in one of his most beloved forms, as a baby (Balakrishna) crawling to steal and eat a large ball of butter. His most popular image, however, is as a young cowherd playing a flute (*Venugopala*), usually accompanied by an image of the young maiden Radha (in many places also viewed as a form of Lakshmi) standing in rapt adoration.

MYSORE, KARNATAKA

Hindus believe that the God Vishnu has had many incarnations. Most famous among them are the Lords Rama and Krishna. Although there are many temples that focus on these and other incarnations, many followers state that the magnificence of Vishnu is so far beyond human conception that only his feet are approachable. The primary image in many temples is carved stone feet that can be touched for darshan with the God.

Love and faith in Vishnu, and especially in his avatar as Krishna, is particularly focused within the Bhakti movement, whereby worshippers become "disciples of devotion." They believe in salvation through the grace of God, that by constantly expressing their deep and abiding love for him they will be rewarded with a blissful life and, eventually, release from rebirth. Although practitioners of Bhakti are everywhere in India, it is particularly popular in certain regions of the country. Twice each year more than one hundred thousand Bhakti worshippers of Vithoba (also called Panduranga), a manifestation of Krishna, gather to walk for fifteen days to his temple in Pandharpur in the central-western state of Maharashtra. Each large group carries with it palanquins on which rest the ceremonial *padukas* (sandals) of a revered saint. Each of these saints, many of them famous poets, also walked the same route. By carrying with them the saints' sandals, and by continuously singing their *bhajanas* (devotional poetry) to Vithoba, the pilgrims believe that they are accompanied by the saints' spirits. These great men and women decried the hierarchy and social prejudice in the orthodox Hinduism of their day. The Bhakti that they espoused joined all people in the worship of Krishna. The pilgrimage brings together Hindus from all castes and occupations. It is a time of brotherhood and great joy, of communal singing and prayer.

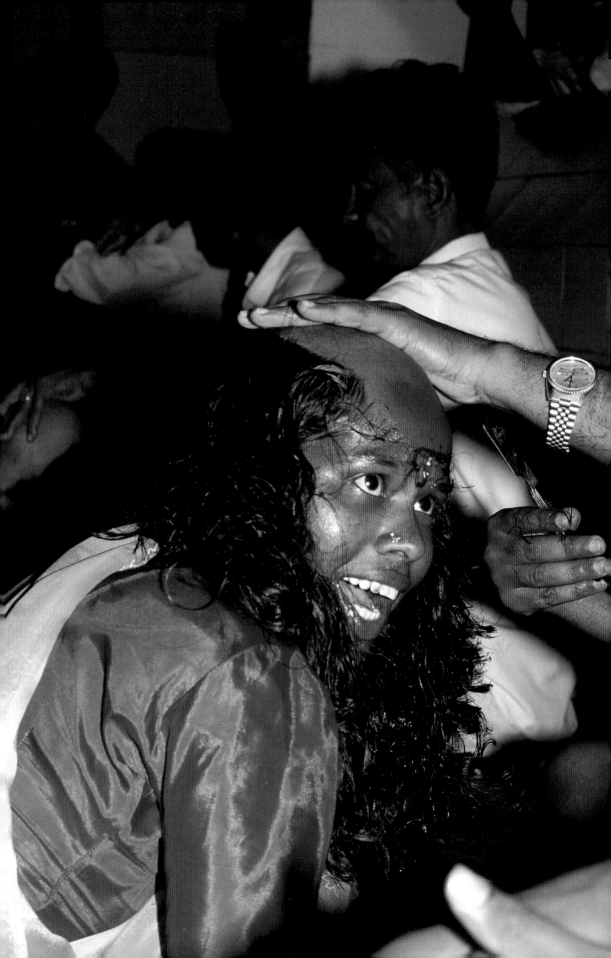

The roads are lined with spectators, particularly near Pandharpur, all straining to touch the padukas and the feet of the pilgrims, thereby having darshan with the saints and with the sacred spirits of these dedicated devotees. They even collect the dust from under the pilgrims' feet, mixing it with a black powder considered sacred to Vithoba and marking their foreheads with it. When the pilgrims reach Pandharpur they culminate their long journey in pujas to Vithoba. In the inner sanctum, each bows to the floor to touch the feet of the God, expressing in this act unconditional surrender before the pervasive power and loving goodness of the Divine.[17]

Although many temples pay tribute to Vishnu's manifestations as Rama and Krishna, the richest temple in India is dedicated to his primary form. In the Tirumala Devasthana in Tirupati, in the southern state of Andhra Pradesh, devotees believe that any wish made in front of the image of Vishnu, known in this temple as Shri Venkateshwara or Balaji, will be granted. Tirupati is the most popular pilgrimage point in the world, more so even than Mecca or Rome, with an average of thirty thousand arrivals each day of the year. The truly dedicated begin their approach to the temple at the base of Tirumala Hill, entering the first of seven tall white gopurams to climb more than ten thousand steep steps. Each step is accompanied by prayers, and each major level by another gopuram: all proper preparation for the darshan to come.

TIRUMALA, TIRUPATI, ANDHRA PRADESH

Worshippers of Vishnu believe that pure communication with God can be achieved through selfless love, devotion, and self-sacrifice. To demonstrate their humility, thousands of pilgrims to one of the God's most important temples have their heads shaved as they arrive.

On top of the hill is an entire small city of temple buildings, mostly lodges, guest houses, dormitories, and eating halls for the devotees. The temple provides more than twenty thousand balanced vegetarian meals daily free of cost to any who desire them, but there are also restaurants. After registering and finding a place to stay, one of the first things that most pilgrims do is have their heads shaved as a sign of humility and sacrifice to the God. The hall of barbers is enormous, often shaving twenty thousand men, women, and children a day; the newly bald heads are painted with yellow sandalwood paste to prevent rashes. If time permits, the devotee then will join the long line to enter the temple, purchasing on the way offerings of coconuts, bananas, sugar, marigolds, and roses. Vendors sell small votive reliefs, made of silver alloy, each embossed with a different human body part. An ailing worshipper might buy, for example, the representation of a foot if he is lame or a pair of breasts if she has been diagnosed with breast cancer. These will be given with offerings of money to Vishnu in hopes of being cured.

Waiting in lines filled with busloads of couples, large families, and the elderly can last five to twelve hours; but on busy festival days it can take more than a day to reach the sanctum. (For thirty rupees, just under one U.S. dollar [though still expensive to many devotees], one can buy a special ticket and pass the bulk of the line and enter within only a couple of hours.) While in line the devotees chant the names, mantras, and prayers of Lord Venkateshwara. After hours of winding back and forth in caged channels, one reaches the main entrance, its columns lined with the stone and bronze statues of the kings and queens who helped to build and renovate the temple. The gopuram leading into the court-yard of the temple is plated with solid silver depictions of Vishnu and his ten avatars. At this stage, the emotions of the devotees are almost at fever pitch; and they chant loudly as they catch their first glimpse of the temple. Inside, the line passes by the offices of the treasury, where dozens of temple employees sort through tall mounds of cash, coins, and gold and silver jewelry that are con-stantly replenished by more baskets full of offerings. All of this income is derived from donations, as well as from the set fees for specially arranged pujas, facilities that are similarly provided at most large temples. The immense wealth of Tirumala (the daily income from donations is the equivalent of U.S. $6 mil-lion!) is used to care for its sixteen thousand full-time employees, to cover the room and board of its many visitors, and to fund numerous hos-pitals, clinics, hospices, colleges, and schools throughout India.

On the granite platform that surrounds the square marble temple, some devotees, overcome by emotion, make a last cir-cumambulation by rolling on their sides around the entire building, their hands held out in prayer toward the inner sanc-tum. The crowds, pushing urgently to enter the doorway, part to let these rolling disciples pass, honoring this act of piety. Priests stream back and forth bearing supplies: large containers of ghee with which to refuel the lamps inside, baskets of offerings to be sorted, huge bronze vessels filled with freshly cooked prashad.

MYSORE, KARNATAKA

Most primary images in the sanctums of Hindu temples cannot be pho-tographed. It would be considered sacrilegious and demeaning to do so. Venkateshwara (Vishnu) in the tem-ple of Tirumala is no exception; but copies of his image are in worship in household shrines throughout India, such as the framed image at the top of this shrine in the home of an actor.

Finally, the devotees reach the inner sanctum to give their names and offerings to the priests, to whisper their special wishes to God, and to see and be seen by Shri Venkateshwara himself. For the God, the darshan is intuitive: his eyes are closed because, it is said, the power of his open gaze would enflame the uni-verse. The image is of tall black stone, standing with his right hand raised in a sign of blessing and his left hand at his side. Vishnu wears a jeweled turban, priceless necklaces, and encrusted gold footwear, while the rest of his body is covered with garlands of marigolds and roses. Many of the devotees are speech-less with wonder, overcome with spiritual ecstasy. Dazed, they allow themselves to be pushed outside and into the courtyard, where some sit a while in the carved colonnade to one side. After resting, they move into the outer courtyard to receive servings of hot sugary rice porridge: prashad blessed by Venkateshwara himself. As they eat the food and leave the temple to return to their lodgings, they feel confident that their requests will be answered and this long pilgrimage was worthwhile.

SIX

Ajay, tired but proud, continues to beat a constant rhythm on the clay drum tied to his waist by a cord. Two other drummers accompany him on larger metal- and brass-encased drums. After a minute of rumbling percussion, Ajay's father, Ramesh, raises his eight-foot-long brass horn to his lips and blasts out another long note to echo through the canyon walls surrounding them. Together they herald the procession of Shiva, Parvati, and Nagamata, the village Goddess, on their annual journey out of the mountains and down to the sacred city nestled in the foothills.

It is a time of great celebration and joy, eagerly anticipated throughout the long, snowbound days of winter. This is the first time that Ajay, just thirteen, has been invited to accompany the entourage. A week ago the preparations and special pujas at the small wooden temple began in their high mountain village. There the ancient stone images of the God and the two Goddesses have not been moved since they were installed long before the first records were made. Each year for many centuries the spiritual energy of these deities has been ceremonially transferred into silver and brass masks to be carried in their place on this special occasion. Three days ago, the masks, bejeweled and garlanded with flowers, were affixed to a tall palanquin surmounted by a large silver umbrella and wrapped in brilliant red and gold brocaded silk. Two long poles were strapped to each side and hoisted onto the shoulders of four village men. It is considered a great honor to be asked to carry the Gods, just as it is to be the musicians who herald their parade. Ajay and the other drummers began pounding out rhythms with their sticks as Ramesh trumpeted the procession of the Gods out of the temple grounds, through the village streets, and down the long trail to the lowlands. Joining them were the temple priest and many of the other villagers. The entire group moved slowly down the

PRECEDING PAGES

MANDAWA, JHUNJHUNU DISTRICT, RAJASTHAN

Images of the Goddess Gauri and her consort, Gan (Parvati and Shiva), are carried through the streets in procession once each year for the Gangaur Festival in Rajasthan.

OPPOSITE

MANDI, HIMACHAL PRADESH

The blare of trumpets and pounding of drums herald the arrival of processional images brought down to the plains from their temples in high Himalayan villages.

mountain, stopping to rest frequently, each stop accompanied by prayers and songs led by the priest. Often they were approached by people along the route: farmers, goatherds, and wood-carriers who would come to give small offerings and receive the blessings of Shiva, Parvati, and Nagamata. They spent two nights on the way, camping in a circle of protection around this movable shrine, awed by their proximity to the images and the responsibility it entailed.

Now they are on the last leg of their journey. They have had a short rest and are ready to make their entrance into the city and the festival grounds. The four men raise the palanquin onto their shoulders; Ajay and the drummers begin their roll; and the full, deep sound of Ramesh's horn bounces off the sides of the mountains. The whole company descends down the last section of path and into the crowded urban streets. Right at the front, Ajay proudly marches alongside his father, loudly drumming while Ramesh blows one resounding note after the other. The crowds part to let them through, each person's hands held up in prayer before the Gods. At last they reach the huge field in the center of the city where the festival takes place. Tens of thousands of people are assembled and, with them, all the tradesmen who cater to their needs: hawkers selling their wares, clothes merchants, games vendors, food sellers, operators of carnival rides, magicians, and astrologers. With great fanfare the entourage approaches the sacred section of the grounds. They are guided into a place prepared for them, and, with a final drum roll and blast of the horn, the men set down the palanquin in the spot where it will stay for the next seven days. The horn and drums are placed alongside it. Nearby is a similar palanquin from another Himalayan village arrayed with its own masked images of Gods and Goddesses, and beyond it another and another stretching out in two long rows.

MANDI, HIMACHAL PRADESH

As the primary images in temples cannot be moved, for special occasions substitutes are created by sculptors so that divine energy may be invoked into them. In mountain villages these processional images are masks sculpted in brass, silver, or gold and tied to elaborately decorated palanquins for transportation. Once they have reached their destination on the plains, they are set up in a public place for worship.

Each is slightly different from the next, containing representations of the major deities and gramadevatas worshipped in each community.

The village priest sits in front of the portable shrine, the four men on each side. Devotees from the city and from other rural villages come down the row, giving a few coins to each shrine and having darshan with each of the many deities. In this way they can have the blessings of many aspects of the Divine all in one place. When a worshipper wants a special blessing and is willing to pay the extra rupees required for this service, the four men pick up the palanquin, sway it from side to side, and allow it to dip to touch the devotee. This action is believed to bring special merit and even to heal negative conditions or diseases.

MANDI, HIMACHAL PRADESH

It is considered auspicious during puja to touch these divine masks, thereby receiving sacred energy into the body.

Several times during the day, Ajay, the two other drummers, and Ramesh play a fanfare to herald the shrine as it is carried on a circuit of the grounds. For the rest of his stay there, Ajay is free to visit the other shrines, to play with newfound friends, and to explore the constantly changing activities of the festival. For seven days he will have the best time of his entire life.

And then the day will come to return. Concluding pujas will be made and the palanquin picked up for the last time. With a final cacophonous circuit of the festival area, the procession will climb the trail out of the city and into the mountains toward the village. But by then Ajay's mind will be filled with stories to tell his friends and his younger brothers and sisters at home—enough to fill the long days and nights until he can again accompany the Gods on their journey to the lowlands next year.

Once each year processions bearing the portable shrines of the Gods converge on sacred towns in the foothills and valleys of the state of Himachal Pradesh in northwestern India. Each region has its own festival in a different time of the year: in the area surrounding Mandi the festival is Shivaratri, celebrated in the Hindu month of Phalguna (mid-February to mid-March); and in the Kulu Valley it is Dussehra, honored in the month of Ashvina (September–October). Local customs dictate to which festival each town and village owes its allegiance. For many, this celebration will be the high point of the year: a chance to emerge from isolated hamlets to meet relatives and friends, exchange news, replenish supplies, and enjoy themselves. But it is also a time of great spiritual import. The festival is an opportunity to share the grace and power of one's own deities with the broader public (as each manifestation of a God or Goddess is believed to have its own unique qualities). A villager gains merit by accompanying his or her deity on this annual journey, just as the worshippers of Vishnu (see Chapter 5) believe that they are spiritually enriched by accompanying the sandals of the saints on pilgrimage. Furthermore, it is considered particularly auspicious to be able to have darshan with each of the portable images from other communities that are assembled in one small area. Most Hindus believe that the concentrated power of these images can enlighten the devotee, transforming misfortune and creating positive dynamic change.[1]

Images from tens of thousands of shrines and temples throughout the Indian subcontinent are paraded through the streets of their environs once each year. Like those in Himachal Pradesh, most primary images in worship cannot be moved. Even if it were physically possible to carry the icon out of the womb chamber of its temple, it would be considered sacrilege to do so. For this reason, most temples have a secondary image for each of the primary deities worshipped within its precincts. This processional image, called an *utsava murti*, is usually cast in bronze, and its form, strictly regulated according to the ancient scriptures, may be quite different from that of the primary image. For example, the icon in a temple to Shiva is almost always a stone Linga, while his utsava murti usually shows one of the God's many other attributes, perhaps as Nataraja (Cosmic Dancer) or Dakshina Murti (Great Teacher). Similarly, the utsava murti of Vishnu may portray any of his ten avatars, such as Varaha (the Cosmic Boar) or Narasimha (the Lion). During the rest of the year, when they are not in use, these bronze sculptures are stored away from the center of the temple, although in some temples they are enshrined within the sanctum. Grouped behind bars for security and dimly lit, they may be observed by devotees as they circumambulate the central shrine. Occasionally they will be given small offerings of fruit, flowers, or coins, but generally they are simply acknowledged as symbols of something yet to come.

PRECEDING PAGES
MUMBAI (BOMBAY),
MAHARASHTRA

Many religious processions are joyous occasions in which the entire community participates. These boys are singing the praises of the God Ganesha during his annual festival.

OPPOSITE
MANDI, HIMACHAL PRADESH

The joint limited resources of the few families living in a Himalayan hamlet mean that they are unable to afford an elaborate palanquin for their Gods. This simply adorned basket suffices as a means for transporting their processional images.

Most of the large bronze images of Hindu deities displayed in museum collections were originally utsava murtis. Because no sacred image may be worshipped once it has been damaged, whether through deterioration or accidental breakage, damaged sculptures are often discarded. In the past, many such images were ritually buried or thrown into temple tanks (reservoirs), from which they have been excavated in the past two centuries to be sold to foreign dealers and museums.[2] Replacement images are cast according to careful prescription and then consecrated in elaborate rituals to transfer the respective deity's sacred energy to this new receptacle. Indeed, the art of image production is as vital in India today as it has ever been.[3]

## FESTIVALS

Each temple has one or more annual festivals in which its utsava murtis are paraded for public viewing in the community. The dates are assigned by traditional preference and reaffirmed yearly by astrological calculations. The size and grandeur of the festivals depend on the relative wealth and popularity of the temple.

PURI DISTRICT, ORISSA

A bronze image of the God Krishna is carried by villagers on a circuit of their community during the annual Dola Purnima Festival. It is considered a great honor to be chosen to carry the festooned palanquin.

Small rural temples may have festivals that last only one to three days, during which time the processional image of the deity is ceremonially carried in a circuit of the community. For example, the Dola Purnima Festival is celebrated in the Hindu month of February–March throughout coastal Orissa. Within the small temple of Krishna in the village of Balipatna are two complementary images of the God, one of permanent, immovable stone, the other of bronze. Throughout the year both are honored with daily pujas. On this special day, the bronze utsava murti is washed with holy water and five sacred substances before being dressed in bright red silk and adorned with gold jewelry. The God is then reverentially placed in a simple carved teak shrine that has been wrapped in brightly colored appliquéd silks and cotton. The deity and the entire shrine are profusely garlanded with flowers. Two poles tied to the sides of the shrine are then picked up by eight young men who triumphantly carry it through the village, stopping at each home for darshan, the receiving of offerings, and the giving of prashad. The deity is then carried out of the village in a long circuit to bless the fields and outlying lands owned by the community's inhabitants. Finally the shrine is returned to the edge of the village to a special platform on which is erected a large swing. The priest then asks the God if he would like to swing. The image is then carefully placed on the swing and rocked back and forth to the accompaniment of musicians and traditional songs celebrating this age-old rite of spring.[4] It is a happy occasion, the crowds laughing and cheering the ritual. It is considered particularly auspicious to have darshan with the God as he is immersed in such pleasure. When this ritual is finished, the God is again invited to enter the portable shrine, which is hoisted onto the shoulders of eight more men and carried back to the temple. A final puja takes place after he is reseated in the spot where he is normally worshipped.

Many large temple complexes, such as those in the far south, observe long and elaborate festivals for their deities. Some temples are very rich, their deities having accrued great wealth from centuries of grateful donors. Each Hindu recognizes that a temple's wealth is entirely dependent on gifts, underlining the concept of reciprocity that permeates all beliefs. The poor have always given what they can in return for the boons that they have received, but throughout history kings and affluent merchants and landowners have shown their gratitude by donating new buildings and images, costly jewelry and clothing, and the sumptuous paraphernalia used in worship. Festivals are the most appropriate time to display this opulence. The temple is transformed into a glittering showcase of the power and magnificence of the Gods, physical proof to the thousands of attendees of the generosity of the Gods in granting wishes. Gods and Goddesses are treated like royalty, resplendent in fabulous silks and ornaments, seated on magnificent thrones, their temples palaces to their regal splendor.

SRI RANGAM, TIRUCHIRAPPALLI, TAMIL NADU

A large gold-plated brass horse holds on its back an elaborately bejeweled bronze image of the God Vishnu during his annual procession outside the temple. Thousands of expectant devotees are packed along the route for hours, waiting to have darshan with the deity.

Hinduism, as has been stated, rests on a foundation of personal relationships with the Gods. It is a religion that encourages the active involvement and participation of every person. While the shrine is the center of the home, the temple is the center of the community, its Gods and Goddesses inseparable from the nature of the community itself. Festivals provide a sense of identity and unity for each member of society, regardless of family, income, or position. They meld personal needs with communal awareness. The temple may be seen in a very real way as an extension of the individual. Its activities are directly related to the character and personality of the devotee. The transfer of the deity from the inner sanctum to the street, from the dark womb of the temple in the center of the city to the thronged parameters of its businesses and residences symbolizes the opening of the heart and mind of each individual through participation in this annual celebration. For a country where much of the population lives near the poverty line, these festivals enable devotees to share in the wealth and glory of their Gods. In many ways community abundance, and its consequent reflection in the wealth and grandeur of its temples and festivals, is viewed as personal abundance. It may be argued that most Hindus experience poverty differently from many in the West. For them the deities and their individual personalities are very real and approachable, and the opulent celebration of the Gods is a vicarious extension of the devotees themselves. The more extravagant the festival, the better it is.

The festivals organized by large temples are often prolonged affairs, lasting a week or ten days. Processions may be conducted morning and evening or even several times a day. In wealthy temples the image of the deity will have its own sets of jewelry, one for each procession. While the jewelry is usually sumptuous, in some temples it is fabulous, given to the deities centuries before by grateful kings and queens.[5] The clothing of the utsava murti is new for each parade. Affluent devotees compete to donate the most magnificent attire, often beautifully woven gold brocades. In many temples the primary deities will be represented in different forms at each procession, which means that each deity has several or even many utsava murtis. Some of these are ancient, others recently cast. All are so covered with clothing, ornamentation, and garlands of

flowers that it can be difficult to discern their distinctive attributes. Furthermore, the utsava murtis may be placed on different vehicles for each procession. Some are pulled in carved wooden carts that can be as large as small temples. Others stand or sit on animal mounts sculpted in wood and covered with silver or even gold! The streets surrounding the temples will be packed with devotees who are participants, not merely observers. Many will comment on the particular beauty of the deity: "Doesn't she look elegant this morning?" or "Isn't he especially handsome this evening?" A poorly adorned image would reflect badly upon the temple and the community and, by extension, upon the devotees.

Every major temple in India celebrates one or more festivals each year. Processions take place every day during the ten-day Brahmotsatvam Festival in the month of March–April at the Kapalishvara Temple dedicated to Shiva in Chennai (Madras). Although one primary image is used repeatedly in several of the parades, some require specific forms of the God and their own particular bronze utsava murtis. For each occasion the deity is dressed in distinctive apparel and jewelry. Devotees eagerly anticipate being able to have darshan with one particular aspect of the Divine and see the famous set of jewels associated with it. The *vahanas*, or vehicles, of the God are different for each procession. Most are created of highly ornate silver. Some are carried on the backs of devotees, while most rest on carts pulled through the streets.

An unusual form of Shiva's bull mount, Nandi, carries the bronze image of the God during the sunrise procession on the third day of the festival. The huge silver-plated wooden sculpture depicts Nandi with a four-armed human body and a bull's head. In the predawn morning the utsava murti is bathed and dressed in

a blue silk tunic, a white dhoti, a profusely jeweled turban, and many necklaces. Then, in an elaborate puja, Shiva is invoked to enter the sculpture, whereupon a group of priests carry the God out of the sanctuary and place him on Nandi's shoulders. Shiva is then garlanded with gigantic ropes of pink roses and white tuberoses. Dozens of priests and specially chosen devotees hoist the long poles that support the enormous weight of Shiva and Nandi onto their shoulders and carry the palanquin out of the eastern gate of the temple. A cry thunders from thousands of waiting worshippers as they emerge, each eager to have darshan with the deity. The procession moves slowly in a circular motion on the streets that surround the temple, stopping often to receive offerings of flowers, coconuts, bananas, and camphor. Priests sitting at Nandi's feet perform ongoing pujas, lighting the camphor arati and giving out sacred ash and prashad to the clamoring devotees. Once Shiva has returned to the eastern gate he is carried inside the compound and invited to return his energy to the primary image.

MYLAPORE, CHENNAI (MADRAS), TAMIL NADU

This bronze processional image of a seated Shiva is elegantly dressed and adorned with sumptuous jewels before being placed upon the back of a gigantic silver Nandi (bull). As the assemblage is slowly pulled through the streets on a wooden cart, Brahmana priests at Nandi's feet conduct pujas on behalf of the throngs of devotees. Photograph by Dick Waghorne.

The process takes place twenty times during the festival—each is similar to but different from the last. Shiva in a variety of forms is shown riding in a tree, on the sun, on the moon, on the back of a demon, on the shoulders of an ascetic, once again upon Nandi (this time in his usual four-legged bovine form), on an elephant, in a huge wheeled chariot, on a horse, and seated above the ten heads of the archdemon, Ravana. Each time the streets are crowded with worshippers, all urgently striving to have darshan with this specific aspect of the Divine.[6]

Perhaps India's most famous festival procession is held annually in the sacred city of Puri in Orissa. In the month of June–July, three immense wooden chariots carry the wooden images of Lord Jagannatha (a form of Krishna), his brother Balabhadra, and his sister Subhadra. The largest chariot, measuring forty-five feet high with sixteen wheels, each seven feet in diameter, is reserved for Jagannatha. The other two are only slightly smaller. All three resemble small temples; they are shaped like the spires under which the images normally reside and are modeled to resemble cosmic mountains. The three simply carved wooden images of the two Gods and Goddess are not utsava murtis. They are the primary images in permanent worship within the sanctum of the temple. In a ritual rare among Hindu temples, these images are brought out of the womb chamber and installed in the chariots. Four thousand temple employees are privileged enough to pull Jagannatha's gigantic vehicle. As many as a million devotees are packed into the streets to witness the spectacle and have darshan with the God. It is even considered auspicious to be crushed beneath the chariot's wheels, this courageous act sanctifying the soul and immediately releasing it from the continuous cycles of rebirth.[7]

# Embracing the Ephemeral:
## Transitory Images

SEVEN

Once each year Sunithi welcomes Lakshmi, the Goddess of Abundance and Prosperity, as a guest in her home. She anticipates this great occasion all year long and is excited that it is finally here. She has been getting ready for several days, scrupulously cleaning the entire house and cooking large quantities of special sweet and salty foods. Fruit was purchased just last night in the nearby Madras market: bananas, apples, guavas, limes, and two coconuts. Long before sunrise on the chosen day in the Hindu month of Bhadon (mid-August to mid-September), Sunithi takes a bath in purifying oils, chants her daily prayers, and performs her morning puja at the shrine on the shelf in her kitchen. She sends her granddaughter, Sumangali, to buy fresh flowers at the early morning market. Sunithi goes outside to draw simple kolams with rice powder on the ground in front of the house, another on the steps, one on the verandah, one on a small plank platform inside the house, and one in the center of the living room. Sumangali returns with baskets full of flowers, then helps her mother, Meena, to center a stool on the kolam in the living room and to lift a wooden columned shrine upon it and put a small tiled table in front. All three women decorate the shrine with fresh banana stalks and mango leaves and array the floor in front with baskets and platters of flowers and fruits.

Sumangali watches attentively as Sunithi sits on a chair and takes onto her lap a freshly polished silver pot. Into this pot she places unhusked rice, turmeric, rolled palm leaves, betel leaves, areca nuts, glass bangles, a small new comb, and a little mirror, each a symbolic gift to the Goddess. She then puts a husked coconut into the mouth of the pot and smears it with yellow turmeric. Sunithi unwraps a silver mask of the Goddess, puts a vermilion dot on its forehead and black kohl under its eyes, and hooks it onto the neck of

PRECEDING PAGES
UCHHAPUR, PURI DISTRICT, ORISSA

Women paint all the walls and floors of their home with sacred designs as part of preparations for Lakshmi Puja, in which the Goddess Lakshmi is invited to be present in the house.

OPPOSITE
MYLAPORE, CHENNAI (MADRAS), TAMIL NADU

To prepare her silver image of the Goddess Lakshmi for puja, Sunithi adorns the sculpture with her own jewelry.

the pot over the coconut. She then places this assemblage on the painted wooden plank and dresses the entire vessel with a piece of purple brocaded silk. Mango leaves behind the coconut rise like a collar above the silver face. Sunithi puts coral earrings into the holes in the image's earlobes and her own precious coral and jeweled necklaces around the neck. Finally, she adorns the image with several garlands of flowers—all this while the family carries on its activities around her. Meena and Sumangali help her as they can but also come and go with other duties. Sunithi's husband, Narayan, watches the news on television in the background. Although this ceremony is conducted for the benefit of the entire family, it is exclusively performed by women. Narayan and his son and grandson will participate only in the final moments.

Now all the preparations are finished, and the primary ritual may begin. Sunithi carries the dressed silver image on the wooden plank out the front door to the verandah, where she places it facing east in the center of the sacred diagram. With her left hand she rings a small brass bell while with her right hand she offers first vermilion, then sandalwood, flowers, water, and camphor. As the flame is lighted, the Goddess Lakshmi is believed to enter the image. What only seconds before was a sacred object is now the Goddess herself. With a joyous song to welcome her, Sunithi picks up the plank and carries the Goddess into the home to place her inside the wooden shrine upon a small mound of unhusked rice.

After sitting to the left of the shrine facing north, Sunithi puts a little turmeric powder on a betel leaf and mixes it with water to make a paste, which she forms into a tiny cone. The yellow cone on the leaf, placed on the table in front of the shrine, represents Ganesha, the elephant-headed Remover of Obstacles. As she again rings the bell with her left hand,

Sunithi gives this God offerings of water, sandalwood paste, vermilion, flowers, bananas, incense, and lighted camphor, reciting as she does so a special prayer to seek his blessings so that nothing inauspicious will occur during this ritual.

Finally the true puja to Lakshmi begins. The Goddess is invoked with a song of praise as Sunithi dips a flower into a vessel of holy water and sprinkles her image with it. Lakshmi is also offered vermilion, sandalwood paste, and turmeric. Then an elaborate ritual begins whereby Sunithi sings the 1,008 names of the Goddess, extolling her divine nature and miraculous attributes while placing offerings of flowers at her "feet." The reciting of each name requires that another flower be given to Lakshmi. Only fragrant blooms are used, and the hundreds of blossoms create a large mound that almost obscures the face of the Goddess, spilling out onto the table beneath her. After all the flowers have been offered, bowls of cooked foods are brought out and beautifully arranged on the floor in front of the shrine. First, incense and a butter lamp are lighted, and then the fruits are offered one by one, followed by all the sweet and salty food. A coconut is broken and its sweet water given to Lakshmi. Camphor is lighted in an arati tray and passed in front of her three times. Sunithi's husband, son, daughter-in-law, and two grandchildren have assembled, and they each wave their hands through the flame and touch their eyelids, offering their own flowers to the Goddess and singing a special prayerful song. Everyone prostrates before Lakshmi as a sign of deep humility, and two small lamps are lighted to ward off the evil eye. The ritual is complete. Some of the food, now prashad, is eaten, and a deep sense of peace pervades the family. The Goddess has been appropriately welcomed into the home, honored, and fed. Here she will remain as a divine guest for two magical days.

red spices/ flowers

MYLAPORE, CHENNAI (MADRAS), TAMIL NADU

Once Lakshmi is installed in her temporary shrine, Sunithi sings her praises for two hours, all the while placing more and more flowers upon her image.

At the last stage, when fruit and sweet and salty cooked foods have been offered, Sunithi prostrates herself before Lakshmi in prayer. The Goddess is considered present in the home for the next two days and will be honored accordingly.

That evening a dinner of milk and cooked lentils with coconut is offered to the Goddess. Then neighbors and friends are invited into the home to visit Lakshmi. They praise her beauty and share in eating her prashad. Those with good voices are asked to sing songs dedicated to Lakshmi. The atmosphere is one of high spirits and laughter. Some of the guests invite Sunithi and her family to their homes to see their Lakshmi shrines and to partake of their just-blessed food. The entire festival draws the community together in celebration.

Each meal on the following day is first offered to the Goddess along with a simplified form of the puja. Her position as honored visitor in the home is thus maintained. In the evening the house is filled with friends who were unable to visit the previous night. The atmosphere is similarly joyous. When all but the immediate family have gone, Lakshmi is offered milk, and the lighted arati tray is circled around her three times. Sunithi then shifts the image slightly to the north, saying, "I've been deeply blessed and honored by your gracious presence. Dearest Mother, please visit my home every year and give me the privilege of worshipping you." The act of moving the image signifies the departure of the Goddess. Just before going to bed Sunithi lifts the image (dressed silver pot, coconut, bejeweled mask, and garlands) out of the wooden shrine and places it for the night into a large metal bin of rice. This action ensures that the family will never go hungry. The next morning she removes the sacred object from the rice container, dismantles the assemblage, and puts it away. Sunithi's necklaces are returned to her neck, and the leftover rice will be saved to be cooked on special occasions, when its sacred auspiciousness is deemed important.

MYLAPORE, CHENNAI
(MADRAS), TAMIL NADU
After the puja, neighbors visit for darshan with the Goddess, to sing her praises and to share in eating the blessed foods.

183

Lakshmi pujas, conducted in homes throughout India once each year, are distinctive in each area. Community and family traditions dictate the time of year, the form of ritual, and the type of image employed. For example, women in coastal Orissa paint their entire homes (exterior and interior walls, floors, and verandahs) with symbols associated with Lakshmi. To signify the entrance of the Goddess into the home, her footprints are painted, leading from the street to each of the rooms. The principal room is the most elaborately painted, and on a small wooden dais in its center stands a black terracotta pot daubed with vermilion. Unhusked rice is poured into this vessel, followed by a small black stone that symbolizes the power of the Goddess. The pot is then dressed in red silk and adorned with garlands of marigolds. During the invocation ceremony, as Lakshmi is invited to enter the image and the home, all the women ululate loudly to prevent evil from infecting this sacred event. As in Sunithi's ritual in Chennai (Madras), the Goddess is treated as an honored guest in the home, regularly bathed, adorned, and fed for two days until she is gratefully allowed to depart.

Each Hindu's year is punctuated by many ephemeral rituals that include shrines and images of deities that are created only for the brief duration of worship. Deities are associated with certain auspicious days when their worship is believed to bring special merit. Temporary shrines will be built either within the home or alongside the street. As the purpose of these structures is to honor the Gods, their production is often elaborate and creative. Remarkably beautiful buildings may be designed and constructed only to be torn down a few days later, with all of their elements recycled. The images may be created by the householder, such as the two forms of Lakshmi described above, or they may be purchased in a market or commissioned to be sculpted by a craftsman or artist. In most cases, purchased or commissioned images will be sculpted in unfired clay, as they are intended to be ritually dissolved by immersion in water when the pujas are complete.

Recycling is a concept essential to traditional Hinduism. Until only a few years ago, nothing was wasted. Paper, scrap metal, and heavy plastics were never discarded; they were reused. The only litter was sewage and sludge. A pervasive attitude suggested that products of the earth should eventually be returned to the earth, which is envisioned as a Goddess who must be honored. Contemporary mass production of plastics and other cheap, nonbiodegradable substances has distorted that ethic, and today the streets of India are increasingly littered with accumulated waste.[1] However, the recycling ethic still affects the creation of temporary abodes for the Gods. Hindus take pride in the fact that every aspect of these shrines is recycled.

PRECEDING PAGES

UCHHAPUR, PURI DISTRICT, ORISSA

Women join together to paint the walls, verandah, and tulasi (sacred basil) planter outside their home with designs auspicious to the worship of Lakshmi during her annual festival.

OPPOSITE

PUNE, MAHARASHTRA

Temporary shrines may be simple or highly elaborate. Here, an immense temporary shrine has been built of recyclable materials to house the ephemeral image of the God Ganesha during his annual festival. Devotees stand for hours in line to be able to sit for the duration of a special puja to Ganesha. Behind them, others wait for their chance to pray.

Many festivals and holy days punctuate every Hindu's yearly calendar. Basant Panchami is a day during the Hindu lunar month of Magh (January–February) when, in central and northern India, Saraswati, the Goddess of Learning, the Arts, Dance, and Music, is honored. Saraswati is envisioned as a beautiful woman dressed in white or yellow, riding a white swan and carrying in her four hands a *veena* (a lutelike instrument), a book, and prayer beads. Although many families have their own particular pujas to this Goddess on Basant Panchami, either within their permanent household shrines or in ones created expressly for this purpose, her most elaborate ceremonies take place in temporary community shrines. Weeks ahead of time, a drive will be organized to raise funds to construct the best possible shrine. Local craftspeople, artists, and other creative members of the community will be consulted and employed to design an innovative structure using whatever materials are available: wood, paper, cloth, leaves, flowers, clay, bricks, metal sheeting, and even glass. Markets are filled with mass-produced images of Saraswati to choose from, but if the funds allow, a sculptor will be commissioned to fashion a special image for the occasion. This image will be installed in the shrine by a priest, who invokes the presence of the Goddess and then conducts pujas to her throughout the day and evening. Depending on local tradition, the image may be kept here for up to four days of continuous ceremonies before a final ritual invites Saraswati's departure. Then the image will be carried in procession to a nearby water source (a reservoir, pond, river, or the ocean) and, with great glee, flung into the water, where it quickly dissolves. In the minds of the devotees, the remaining energy of the Goddess is absorbed through the river back into the cosmos, and the festival is complete. The shrine itself will be dismantled and its elements recycled.

CALCUTTA, WEST BENGAL

An unfired clay image of Saraswati, the Goddess of Learning, the Arts, Dance, and Music, waits in her temporary urban shrine in order that her devotees might have her darshan.

KHONANT, KURDHA DISTRICT, ORISSA

Offerings of puffed rice have been given to this village image of Saraswati. In honor of the Goddess, the priest is building a *homa* (sacred fire) on a diagram of colored earth.

As the Goddess of Learning, Saraswati is particularly associated with schools and children. Classes join together to prepare for their own Saraswati Puja, each student contributing his or her talents to create the most elaborate shrine. Basant Panchami begins with ritual prayers in school thanking the Goddess for her help during the previous year and asking for her aid in opening the doors to future learning. Then a holiday is declared, and many children celebrate the rest of the day by flying kites. It is considered auspicious to wear yellow and to eat the yellow foods specially cooked in every home only on this day and first offered to Saraswati. The next morning, following a brief, final puja, the children assemble before class to carry their image of the Goddess for their own immersion ceremony.[2]

Many Hindu rituals similarly include the immersion and dissolution of an unfired image at the end of the ceremony. This process is a natural extension of the entire concept of birth, death, and rebirth that applies to every aspect of the cosmos. Hindu mythology refers to many stories of the continuous cycles of creation and destruction. The universe is created, it exists for several eons, and then it is destroyed, only to be created again in a new form. Every part of the cosmos has its own spirit, its period of existence, its death, and its reincarnation. This continuity of change applies even to the Gods themselves. The recycling of natural elements in rituals is an obvious symbol of one of the primary principles of Hindu belief. It reminds the devotee of the continuous processes of change that affect the entire universe.[3]

## SURYA

The festival of the sun, Chhattha, is celebrated twice each year, during Kartika (October–November) and Vaishakha (April–May), in the eastern Gangetic Plain. Surya, the Sun God, is worshipped for his omniscient clarity and his healing power. Large communities pool their resources to commission potters to sculpt elaborate dioramas depicting Surya driving his chariot through the heavens, often accompanied by numerous attendants. The potters first build for each figure a framework of sticks wrapped with straw applied with thick clay. They then delicately sculpt the clay into likenesses of the solar deity, the horses that draw his chariot, and his attendants. Finally, each sculpture is painted in brilliant colors, topped with wigs, and dressed in sumptuous clothes where appropriate. They will be installed in a temporary roadside shrine for eight days of worship. On each predawn festival day devotees throng alongside the nearby Ganges River to immerse themselves and greet the rising sun with prayers and baskets of offerings before they proceed to the shrine for pujas. After a final ritual on the ninth day, the images are carried in procession to the banks of the river; the wigs, clothes, and jewelry are removed and the elaborate sculptures ceremoniously thrown in. The next morning all that remains to remind the riverside bathers of this festival are the images' straw-wrapped skeletons washed up on the banks.[4]

PATNA, BIHAR

A potter lovingly sculpts a large unfired clay image of the Sun God, Surya, in preparation for the Chhattha Festival. Once the image has dried, it will be painted in brilliant polychrome colors, dressed, and placed in a tented temporary shrine at a main intersection for the entire community to worship.

## MANIFESTATIONS OF PARVATI

During the month of Chaitra (March–April) the women of each farming family in Rajasthan conduct ritual prayers in their fields to Gauri, a form of Parvati worshipped as the Goddess of Agricultural Prosperity. On the first day they create a temporary shrine in their homes, conduct a short puja to the Goddess, and then proceed to their fields. There they sculpt five crude mud and cowdung images of the Goddess, which they put into a small terracotta pot; in another pot they plant

191

millet seeds. Then they sing the praises of Gauri and request her aid in ensuring the health of their crops and of the members of their families. On each of the following eighteen days of the festival they return to the fields to water the sprouting seeds and pray to the Goddess. On the final day, when the millet has grown into tall seedlings, they carry the two vessels back to the temporary household shrine, symbolically bringing Gauri's divine energy into the home, where they conduct a puja with songs and offerings. Then, in procession, the women of each house in the community carry their sacred vessels to the town center, where a wooden image of Gauri and her consort, Gan (an aspect of Shiva), are installed. They each press forward to have darshan with the deity, leaving the millet seedlings as gifts. When this puja is finished they carry the pot containing the mud and cowdung images to a local water source, sing final tributes, and pour the sculptures into the water. The Goddess has been honored, her assurance of bountiful crops and good health requested, and all that has been created from the earth has been returned to it. The cycle is complete.[5]

SIKAR, RAJASTHAN

In order to celebrate Durga Puja in a manner traditional to their culture, a group of Bengalis living in western India has commissioned a local artist to sculpt images of Durga, Ganesha, and other deities in unfired clay. Offerings such as this garland of marigolds will be given throughout the nine-day festival.

Durga, the great Warrior Goddess, is another manifestation of Parvati. She represents the lethal energy of feminine anger when turned against evil. Hindu legend states that when the world was under attack by the worst of all demons, the buffalo Mahisha, the male Gods were immobilized by fear. They consequently joined forces to endow Durga with all of their powers, symbolized by her multiple arms, each carrying a different God's weapon. Riding a lion into battle, she destroyed the buffalo demon and saved the world, thereby exemplifying the ultimate power (Shakti) of the feminine. Her many devotees believe that Durga destroys illusion and challenges mankind in his complacency. She, like her other form as Kali, is the most demanding of deities—but she is also loved by her devotees. Through the ashes of her destruction she creates new life and fresh hope. Durga is viewed as the dynamic, transformative power of the benign Goddess Parvati, wife of Shiva.

MANDAWA, JHUNJHUNU DISTRICT, RAJASTHAN

On the final and eighteenth day of the Gangaur Festival, women from every household congregate in the center of town to give offerings to the Goddess Gauri.

Although Durga Puja is a daily occurrence for many Hindus, it is particularly celebrated during the nine-day annual festival of Navaratri in the month of Ashvina (September–October). In the northeastern state of West Bengal, huge images depicting Durga riding her lion and killing the buffalo demon are installed once each year on large platforms inside tents. The money to support the creation of these images, the hiring of priests, and the cooking of special foods to be given as offerings is raised in each community by subscription. The consequent pujas to the Goddess are elaborate and intense. Even though Durga's image is intended to be ephemeral and will be destroyed at the end of the festival, devotees are overcome with emotion at being able to have her darshan. Verses commonly sung by women

during this festival describe in detail the visit of the Goddess from her abode in the Himalayas, where she stays with her demanding husband, Shiva. Once each autumn she comes home to Bengal, and the women assume the maternal role of spoiling her with rich foods, entertainment, new clothes, and jewelry. Her visit is compared to the annual visit of Hindu brides to their natal families: a time of joy at the reunion and inevitable sadness in departure. Married women clamor to reach her image so that they might put a little of the powdered vermilion that adorns her into the parts of their hair, a gesture symbolic of solidifying their own strength. On the ninth day, Dussehra, when the image is carried in procession from its platform to be immersed in the Ganges, the Goddess is said to be returning to the mountain palace of her husband. The sense of loss at being parted from Durga's physical presence is so great that many women shed tears on the banks of the river.[6]

## GANESHA

MANDAWA, JHUNJHUNU DISTRICT, RAJASTHAN

One of the rituals of the Gangaur Festival is for the women to sculpt mud into little images of the Goddess which are then kept in terracotta bowls during the eighteen days of prayers. On the final day, after offerings are made to the primary image of the Goddess (shown on the previous page), these dried mud sculptures are thrown into a nearby well, thereby demonstrating the Hindu concept of regeneration and return.

Ganesha, one of the two sons of Shiva and Parvati, is beloved by all Hindus regardless of region, sect, or caste. As the Remover of Obstacles, this elephant-headed God is invoked at the beginning of every endeavor. Before leaving the house, cooking a meal, starting a project, or beginning a performance, a quick prayer will be said to Ganesha to ensure a successful outcome. The first action in almost all Hindu pujas is to honor this God. The focus of the devotion might be to his permanent image (a sculpture, painting, or print) or to a temporary representation, such as the small cone of turmeric created and worshiped by Sunithi at the commencement of her Lakshmi Puja. Ganesha is by far the most common image in India, found in architectural ornamentation, carved in wood or stone, cast in bronze, gold, and silver, fashioned of crystal or jewels, and featured in murals, paintings, prints, and even in advertising. Although numerous temples are devoted primarily to his worship, particularly in southwestern India, most temples to other deities also include small separate shrines to Ganesha so that he might be worshiped first, before one enters the womb chamber. Many poster prints of other Gods include the representation of Ganesha for the same reason.[7]

Although prayers to Ganesha are made daily by most Hindus, his worship is considered particularly auspicious during the festival of Ganesha Chaturthi in the lunar month of Bhadra (August–September). On this day throughout India devotees either will make special homage to their permanent household images of Ganesha or will purchase ephemeral images and erect temporary shrines for the occasion. However, Ganesha Chaturthi is the most important festival of the year in the southwestern Indian states of Maharashtra and Karnataka. Its popularity

CLOCKWISE FROM TOP LEFT

MYSORE, KARNATAKA

The living room of a Brahmana household.

MYSORE, KARNATAKA

The kitchen of the house of a college professor.

MATANGA, MUMBAI (BOMBAY), MAHARASHTRA

The single-room shantytown house of a laborer.

UMRAJ, SATARA DISTRICT, MAHARASHTRA

One of two rooms that make up a lower-middle-class tent-maker's house.

Every year each Hindu household in central-western India purchases its own unfired clay image of Ganesha and places it in a temporary shrine in a place of honor in the home. The shrines are as varied as the types of homes.

was greatly increased during the late nineteenth century, when it was promoted by the anti-British freedom fighter Lokmanya Tilak as a spiritual means for consolidating pan-Indian pride in indigenous culture. Today it joins together more than fifty million people in ten days of unequivocally joyous celebration.

On the first day, each family goes to the market to purchase an unfired clay image of Ganesha. Devotees are encouraged to choose one whose expression delights them. The image could be small and simply adorned or large and elaborate, depending on family resources. It is almost always painted in bright polychrome colors. The ritual that follows varies according to family traditions. Some ask the sculptor to invoke life into the image at the time of purchase by applying pupils to his eyes, thereby facilitating darshan. Others wait for that transformation until the image is installed in their shrines at home. In either case the image will be carried to the house in a happy procession accompanied by music, singing, and laughter. Once there Ganesha will be graciously invited to enter the home to be placed in a temporary shrine created for the occasion, usually in the living room or kitchen. Virtually every household partakes in this process, even those that are almost destitute. If the family is able to afford to celebrate only one festival each year, it will be Ganesha Chaturthi. As the Remover of Obstacles, Ganesha is the one who may improve their future. Once installed in the shrine he will be bathed in a few drops each of sacred substances, offered sandalwood paste, rice grains, and fruits and flowers, adorned with a sacred thread and dressed, presented with lamps, given food, and supplicated with camphor. After this ritual he is considered an honored guest in the home, to be venerated with pujas morning and evening.

SHOLAPUR, MAHARASHTRA

On the tenth and final day, the temporary image of Ganesha is carried from the home in a great procession of joyous dancing and singing. Accompanying one such image is a troupe of Wagha Murali, a special group of devotees to the Goddess Durga who conduct ritual dances as a means of showing their dedication to the Divine.

The length of Ganesha's visit in the home is a family decision: it may be one, three, five, seven, nine, or ten days, although the latter is the most common. On the morning of the final day Ganesha is offered a special breakfast, thanked for the blessings that he has bestowed on the household by his stay, and invited to depart. He is again carried in joyous procession through the streets. If the image is large, he may be pulled in a cart or in a bicycle rickshaw or even carried in a car to a river, pond, or beach, where the last puja will be conducted. Then, with loud shouts of praise, the male members of the family carry his image as far out into the water as possible and throw it in.[8]

During the same festival, most communities in this region pool their resources to create large community Ganesha shrines. The size of the structure and the image within it depend on financial capability. Many images are simply enlarged and colorful versions of those in temples. However, as Ganesha is associated with laughter and whimsy, they may be intended to be humorous. Each year the community prides itself on the creativity of its shrine's design, drawing on the talents

199

of its best artists. Annual competitions may be organized to propose innovative and appealing concepts. The results are thousands of distinctive temporary community Ganesha shrines throughout these two states. Most of these ephemeral community sculptures are large, and some may rise as high as eighteen feet! Subjects may be drawn from well-known legends (for example, Ganesha as a baby being protected by his mother, Parvati, from the rage of his father, Shiva, or as the Lord of Sound dancing upon the tops of the Himalayas). Or they may be based purely upon the imagination of the artist: the God shown driving a clamshell chariot drawn by huge fish or dancing on the head of a cobra that sways out of the basket of a huge snake charmer, or as the lead singer in a band of favorite pop stars. Ganesha has even been shown accompanied by Elvis and Madonna!

The image (or images, if the production is a montage) is commissioned from a local sculptor according to mutually agreed-upon specifications. On the first day of the festival a large group from the community arrives at the artist's studio with a priest to conduct an initial puja. Then they carry the image(s) to a wagon or the back of a truck for the journey to the new shrine. As they near their destination they are joined by crowds, often including a musical band, welcoming Ganesha to his new home. Upon arrival, the image is installed in the shrine by one or more priests with all the attendant rituals; it will remain there for the full ten days of the festival. Pujas are conducted throughout each day, with the largest attendance in the early morning before work and in the evening. The most popular shrines in the large cities, such as Pune and Bombay, may be continuously thronged with devotees.

UMRAJ, SATARA DISTRICT, MAHARASHTRA

Communities throughout the Indian southwest pool resources to commission large temporary images of Ganesha that stand throughout the festival in streetside shrines. Each image is different, its form and decoration dependent on the imagination of the artist. This one has been garlanded in paper currency.

On the tenth day, after a last puja, Ganesha is lifted off his dais and again placed on a wagon or truck bed. Accompanied by most of the community and often by a band, he will begin his long progression toward the water. In principal cities the crowds are enormous—literally millions of people gather in a ponderously slow parade, with throngs transporting each large community image and thousands of families carrying their own household Ganeshas. As the festival usually takes place during the monsoon season, the congestion may be compounded by heavy rain or humid heat. Nevertheless, the benevolence of the God is infectious, and the mood is one of gaiety and celebration. The procession, which might take as long as twelve hours to reach its destination, is remarkably good-humored. In a normal year in Mumbai (Bombay), the nonstop parade of Ganeshas to the Arabian Sea lasts from early afternoon until just before dawn the next day. At the beach the image is stripped of its finery, lifted by dozens of devotees, and ceremoniously carried as far as possible into the churning water before it is allowed to topple into the surf. As Ganesha has been sculpted of unfired clay, his image dissolves rapidly in the water and all of his devotees begin their long walk back home, this year's festivities complete.

For the culmination of the Ganesha
Chaturthi Festival, ephemeral
images of the elephant-headed God,
big and small, community and
household, are carried in procession
to a water source to be immersed
and dissolved. In Mumbai, they are
taken to the sea.

Aside from the many festivals that require the construction of temporary shrines and images, Hindus have many other occasions for creating ephemeral art as a part of religious rituals. Examples already discussed are the decorations that women paint on the walls and floors of their houses as invocations to the deities of abundance and protection. Sacred diagrams are also drawn at the beginning of many pujas, the counterpart to the mandala delineated at the construction of a temple (see Chapter 5). A *yantra* is a symbolic formula of lines used to attract the energy of a deity into a sacred space. For example, before an image may be installed in a shrine, a yantra is incised on a copper plate and buried beneath the womb chamber. In many rituals where a temporary shrine is required, a yantra for a specific deity may be drawn on the ground with either white or colored powders. The resulting design is considered all that is needed for contact with the Gods. The yantra itself, viewed as the linear form of the deity, will then be given the offerings appropriate to a puja. Once the ritual is complete, the diagram either may be destroyed or left to disintegrate in the wind or by abrasion.

Many temple rituals involve the creation of yantras for specific purposes: to pray for the health of a family member or for success in a particular endeavor. In a temple to the Goddess Mariamman in Samayapuram, Tamil Nadu, for example, three young unmarried women join together to create an elaborate yantra, a process that takes six hours. They are each praying to the Goddess for her aid in finding a good and reliable husband, a dependable father for future children. They begin by drawing a huge grid of dots on the granite-paved floor of the central court directly in front of the image of Mariamman. They then laboriously connect the dots with fluid lines by trickling rice flour through their fingers until they create an immense symmetrical lotus with exactly one thousand and eight petals (1,008 is a particularly sacred number in Hinduism). Once the flower is complete they place a small terracotta lamp on each petal, fill it with ghee, and light it. Burning together, all one thousand and eight lamps are a remarkable tribute to the Goddess, proof of the depth of their devotion and a deeply moving invocation to the power of the Divine Feminine. When the yantra has finished burning, it is dismantled. Its value lies solely in its creation and in the link it provides between devotee and deity.

SAMAYAPURAM, TIRUCHIRAPPALLI DISTRICT, TAMIL NADU

As part of her invocation to the Goddess Mariamman for aid in finding a good husband, this woman uses rice flour to paint a 1,008-petaled lotus on the floor of the temple just in front of the sanctum.

With the help of two other unmarried women who are also conducting
this ritual, the young woman puts
out 1,008 clay lamps with wicks, fills
each with ghee, and lights them all.
The extraordinary lotus, symbol of
the Goddess, will burn for about one
hour in the near darkness of the
temple before the ritual is finished.

The news alarmed Kamala. Her little granddaughter was so young, so beautiful. She had known from the moment she was born that she would be the pride of the family, that she would succeed in life. And now they had just been told that there was nothing to be done. Little Aditi, only fourteen months old, was dying of this new strain of cholera, and the doctors were at their wits' end. The family had rushed the delirious, feverish baby to the hospital four days before; yet despite all the care of the medical team, the strong medicines, the intravenous and oxygen, her condition had grown steadily worse.

Kamala prayed with all her concentration focused on Shiva, saying his name again and again, chanting the mantra she had been given when she had come of age, asking the God for his help in this dire emergency. And then, suddenly, she knew what to do. She pushed through all the other family members: her son Pradeep, his wife, Geeta, her two older sons and their wives. She went directly to the bedside, pulled out the needles and tubes from Aditi's tiny arm, took the oxygen mask from her face, and cradled her in her arms. Geeta cried out in protest, reaching for her daughter, as, behind her, the nurse stormed in to stop this action; but Kamala did not relinquish the girl. She firmly told her plan to everyone there. She was taking Aditi to be healed by the Goddess. Parvati would save their child. They were going to the temple at Ochira.

*What!? Gods more powerful than medicine?*

Everyone hurried out of the hospital and down the street toward the bus station. The next bus to Ochira was not for five hours, and they did not have enough money for a taxi. One of the girl's uncles talked a motor rickshaw into taking Kamala, Pradeep, Geeta, the baby, and himself. The others would come later by bus. By pooling all their resources they would just have enough to pay. Even by this transportation it would take almost two hours to reach the temple.

PRECEDING PAGES

OCHIRA, ALAPPUZHA DISTRICT, KERALA

Wooden representations of entire bodies and body parts, originally given as votive offerings, are now used as agents for Divine healing in this sacred tree shrine in southern India.

OPPOSITE

OCHIRA, ALAPPUZHA DISTRICT, KERALA

A wooden image of the Goddess Parvati has been sprinkled with vermilion and turmeric powder as part of prayers for healing.

They crammed themselves into the little vehicle and took off. Together they sang the praises of the Goddess, over and over calling out her name. Little Aditi stayed on Kamala's lap the whole time, her mother constantly applying fresh cloths soaked in cool water to her feverish skin. Finally they pulled up to the temple at Ochira and dismounted from the rickshaw.

Ochira is unique among all Hindu temples. Even though it has been famous throughout the area for centuries for the innumerable miracles that have taken place there, the temple itself is open air. It has the towering gateway common in this southern Indian state of Kerala, and its grounds include a marriage hall and an assembly hall. The large field that constitutes the center of the complex contains two sacred trees and a sacred grove. Local legend states that the trees represent the Absolute Divine, Parabrahman: God without form, unmanifested in any image. It is a place like Lourdes in France, to which the faithful come to be healed.

OCHIRA, ALAPPUZHA DISTRICT, KERALA

Beneath the lateral roots of these ancient entwined trees, wooden votive healing sculptures surround the image of Parvati. When a devotee prays for healing, he or she will pick up one of the votive sculptures and, with it, circle the part of the body that needs healing. For the people of this region, Ochira is like Lourdes, and many miraculous healings take place there.

Kamala knows right where she is going: directly to the back of the first tree. A three-foot-high cement platform surrounds and contains a peepul and a kadamba tree entwined with long gnarly roots at their base. Small open shrines on both sides are facilitated by non-Brahmana priests, who conduct special pujas in the morning and evening and remain throughout the day to receive offerings, give prashad, and advise devotees in the appropriate procedures for approaching Parabrahman. Even though Ochira is maintained as a temple to the unformed Absolute, a wooden image of the Goddess Parvati stands at the rear shrine, installed by a grateful past recipient of healing. Devotees claim that many miracles have occurred here with the aid of the Goddess. It is this image that Kamala saw in her prayers in the hospital. It is here that she has brought her granddaughter to be healed.

First, with the priest's instruction, she pours fresh vermilion and sandalwood powder over the image, placing coins at Parvati's feet. Then she lowers Aditi to the sand beneath the tree. The baby is still delirious, faintly moaning as she feverishly thrashes her head back and forth. Kamala opens her heart and her mind to the Goddess, loudly calling out her name and vowing to undergo arduous annual fasting and penance if the child is cured. Other women, strangers who have been touched by these desperate prayers, crowd around Geeta to ululate in high-pitched rolling cries intended to keep away death. Pradeep and his brother prostrate themselves on the ground, their hands stretched out toward Parvati. The priest chants with his eyes closed. For several minutes all attention is vibrantly focused on the Goddess, all beseeching her intervention, all requesting her aid.

And then Aditi stops twisting her little body and lies still, her breathing regular and her eyes clear. Kamala feels her forehead, loudly proclaims that the fever is gone, and then collapses to the ground, rolling back and forth and chanting: "Amma, Amma, Amma, Amma" ("Mother, Mother, Mother, Mother!"). She is overcome with gratitude to the Goddess. Geeta and Pradeep rush forward and scoop up the little girl in their arms, tears streaming down their cheeks as they realize that she looks changed, tired and pale but no longer ill. They cry out vows to Parvati to honor her for the rest of their lives.

When the family has recovered, they all sit alongside the tree, each alternately picking up the small girl to stroke and kiss her. They wait for the evening puja to join the hundreds of other devotees in prayers to Parabrahman and the extraordinary sacred power manifest in this place. When the rest of their relatives arrive by bus late that night, they all share in adulation for the miracle that has taken place.

OCHIRA, ALAPPUZHA
DISTRICT, KERALA

A baby girl delirious with the critical fever of cholera is placed by her grandmother in front of the image of Parvati. Within seconds her fever has abated and she is entirely healed of the disease.

Offerings of money are placed by grateful devotees in front of votive wooden objects used as aids for healing.

*[handwritten marginalia: OMG→ IS THIS REAL?]*

*[handwritten marginalia: where does karma play in to this? karma can be sort of saved up + used directly in prayer for health, etc]*

One of the underlying popular tenets of Hinduism is the acceptance of miracles. Most Hindus believe that direct appeal for aid from a deity often results in divine intervention. The Gods and Goddesses are approachable and, when properly beseeched, will change the course of events. Prayers for intercession may be made to any deity, the choice entirely dependent on the beliefs and inclinations of the devotee. Stories in every neighborhood revolve around ancestors or acquaintances whose sincere devotion resulted in the prevention of misfortune and disaster. Elements of nature such as certain trees or rocks are believed to possess powerful healing energy. Just touching such an object may result in a miracle.

PRECEDING PAGES

PATNA, BIHAR

A woman lies prostrate on the ground and stretches as far as she can reach to mark the dirt with her fingers. She rises to place her heels on that mark; prays while standing; and then prostrates herself again. In this manner she travels several miles to fulfill a vow to the Sun God, Surya.

OPPOSITE

BEDLA, UDAIPUR DISTRICT, RAJASTHAN

In an ancient ritual that has been conducted on this spot for centuries, devotees in need of healing crawl through an arch of stone and clay at the BedlaMataji Temple. Many claim efficacious cures.

Innumerable examples of such healings exist. For instance, at the BedlaMataji Temple just outside the city of Udaipur in Rajasthan, as many as twenty thousand devotees come for healing during the ten-day Navaratri Festival each year. While making a wish to the Goddess Durga, they crawl through a short U-shaped arch of stone and clay believed to be vibrant with sacred energy. If the individual's prayer is answered, he or she will promise to return to crawl seven more times through the arch before giving substantial offerings to the Goddess. Many devotees claim that this action has resulted in miracles. At the roots of the sacred trees in Ochira, described in the beginning of this chapter, groupings of ancient wooden sculptures represent legs, arms, and complete human figures. Years ago they were placed there to remind Parabrahman of the specific healing requested. When the miracles occurred, the objects were left behind. Devotees believe that these sculptures are now imbued with sacred healing energy. The afflicted will pick up one that pertains to that part of the body that needs attention and revolve it around the spot, accordingly absorbing divine healing.

Physical conditions in the Indian subcontinent are generally much more severe than are those of Europe or North America. Disasters such as floods, famines, and earthquakes are common; the climate makes it a breeding ground for contagious diseases; and overpopulation often makes living conditions oppressive. Hinduism, unlike Western religions, does not separate God from the devil. Both good and evil are viewed as divine. Both are essential parts of existence, their deeper purposes unfathomable to mankind. Shiva is described as both creator and destroyer of the universe. The wrath of his consort, Parvati, in her form as Kali, is said to cause calamities; her anger must be appeased through pujas. She is, however, also viewed as the nurturing mother who lovingly cares for her devotees. Some deities are particularly associated with disease and healing: Sitala is worshipped in northern India as the Goddess of Smallpox, the

219

Provider of Good Fortune, and the Protector of Children, while her counter-part in southern India is known as Mariamman. Each of these Goddesses is believed to be both the cause and the cure of illness. A sick person will be said to be possessed by the Goddess, and special rituals must be enacted to please her, to cool her anger and make her benign. The Goddess within the patient will be offered special foods believed to be her favorites, foods that consequently ease the fever and help to heal the disease.[1]

The first time that newborn babies are taken out of their homes in central Tamil Nadu, usually at three or six months, will be to be blessed by the Goddess. Many babies are brought by their parents to be laid in front of the image of the Goddess in Mariamman's temple in Punalur, near Thanjavur, to ensure that they are protected from harm. So many healing miracles are claimed to have occurred in this temple that it has become remarkably popular. The priests found that the congestion of milling devotees prevented them from being able to conduct normal pujas, so they relegated the more elaborate personal rituals to a side shrine. In a courtyard, the women of each family gather to sing praises to the Goddess as they mix and roll out special sweetened rice and lentil flour balls to be given as part of their offerings for the health of their babies. Other women make special rice cakes mixed with ghee and turmeric that will be placed over the diseased part of a family member's body. A small wick in the center of the cake is lighted as an invocation to Mariamman, who is said to draw out the negative energy from the ill person and heal him or her. Many diseases, including tuberculosis, cholera, and cancer, are believed to be healed in this manner.[2]

**PUNALUR, THANJAVUR DISTRICT, TAMIL NADU**

In a temple to the Goddess Mariamman, a ritual to heal a woman diagnosed with severe cervical cancer includes specially made rice cakes that are placed over the afflicted area and lighted with wicks. The disease, viewed as contamination, is believed to be drawn out through the flames. The numbers of lottery tickets have been scrawled on the back wall for good luck by other devotees.

Cobras, the most poisonous of snakes, are revered as divine agents of healing. A home inhabited by a *naga* (cobra) is believed to be lucky. The snake that is regularly prayed to and fed is said to never harm family members. Many shrines and temples have grown up around the mounds or tree roots where Nagas live, and the snakes there are given daily offerings of milk and eggs. Stone sculptures depicting hooded Nagas, sometimes with a human form beneath the hood, stand beneath many sacred trees, particularly in southern India. Occasionally the image will portray two entwined snakes identical in form to the caduceus, the common symbol of Western medicine. Women usually worship at Naga shrines more often than do men. They make special pujas to the Nagas for fertility and successful childbirth and for the health of family members. In northern India, particularly in the areas of the eastern Gangetic Plain where poisonous vipers abound, Manasa is worshipped as the Goddess of Snakes.

Closely connected with the earth, fertility, and marriage, she is usually depict-ed in human form surrounded by vipers. When someone is bitten by a snake, Manasa is worshipped to draw out the venom.

A divine image, particularly one that has been worshipped for years, may be considered to be so imbued with sacred energy that simply being in its prox-imity will heal disease and reverse misfortune. The longer it has been the object of worship, the more powerful it is believed to be. Many miracles, for example, are cited by pilgrims who have made the long journey to the famous temple of Srinathji (a name for Krishna) in Nathdwara, Rajasthan. They believe that the preparation for such a pilgrimage, the voyage itself, and preliminary rituals after arrival at the temple act as a means of cleansing and readying oneself for being filled with God's grace. In the course of darshan with Srinathji during puja, the undiluted power of God is viewed as purifying, healing any imperfection or misfortune.[3]

The growth of small shrines into large temples, as discussed in Chapter 5, is largely based on the response of grateful devotees to the specific blessings received from the deity associated with that spot. The largest temples in India, such as those of Jagannatha in Puri and Meenakshi in Madurai, among hundreds of others, have gained their popularity purely through their records of achievement, which include innumerable healing miracles. Many devotees returning from pujas in these places claim that their prayers have been answered. Tirumalai, the temple of Vishnu that is the richest pilgrimage center in the world, has gained all of its wealth from donations by grateful devotees. Hundreds of thousands of smaller temples, those in little communities throughout the Indian subcontinent, have their own stories of miracles that have happened in the past as well as in the present.

In general, healing is believed to come to those who deserve it. Disrespectful or inappropriate behavior (for example, the seeking of self-satisfaction at the expense of one's family or friends) is considered to demean the individual char-acter and to create bad karma. Karma, it may be remembered, is based on the absolute law of cause and effect, of total responsibility for one's actions. Karma is the sum of the entire character, the tally of all the good and bad acts in this life and all previous lives. Social or material inequalities are viewed, in part, as the natural product of past-life karma. Each individual is ultimately account-able for every choice, every action, and even every thought. Selfless dedication to the duties in life, to the responsibilities undertaken by being born into this body, this family, and this occupation, are considered to be a virtue, to create good karma. Countless Hindu treatises, legends, and stories extol the virtuous life. Clear-sighted commitment to the fulfillment of duty to family and deity are the highest possible human achievement. Acts of virtue are believed to attract the positive attention and beneficence of the Gods and, when necessary, to clear a path for healing energy.[4]

## VRATA

The purpose of many Hindu rituals is to improve the balance of karma. The properly conscientious Hindu conducts regular pujas, in which the Gods are honored and extolled, as well as samskaras, in which the events of the life cycle (birth, betrothal, marriage, and death, to name a few) are appropriately celebrated. Another common means of clearing the negative karma created by past mistakes in action or judgment is through the fulfillment of a *vrata* (specific vow) to a God or Goddess. A devotee promises the deity that she or he will regularly undergo a certain action that will help to purify body and mind and demonstrate piety. Many vratas are relatively undemanding, usually involving a fast accompanied by intense prayers. A vow will be made that on the one day each week considered auspicious to that particular deity, the devotee will go without solid food from sunrise to sunset. Regional cultures differ in the traditional attributes of each day. In much of northern India, Monday is the day dedicated to Shiva and Lakshmi, Tuesday to Hanuman, Ganesha, and Kali, Wednesday to Vishnu, Thursday to personal deities or to one's guru, Friday to the Goddess in her many forms, Saturday to the Divine in its most powerful aspect (Shiva as the Destroyer or Durga as the All Conquering), and Sunday to Surya. Most Hindus would make a vrata to fast for only one day in the week, although some might make special concessions on another day as part of a second vow (for example, a person who regularly eats meat might vow to Vishnu to eat solely vegetarian food on Saturdays).

MYLAPORE, CHENNAI (MADRAS), TAMIL NADU

Throughout India the cobra is viewed as a deity of healing. Numerous shrines, particularly in the northeast and the south, are associated with the mounds or trees under which cobras live. Women worship at these shrines for successful childbirth and the health of family members.

Any vrata, simple or complex, is a serious commitment to the Divine and must be enacted exactly as it was promised. Failure to do so may result in disaster. Stories abound of dishonored vows and the divine retribution that followed. If someone is incapable of honoring a sacred vow through physical impairment or death, the responsibility may be assumed by another member of the family. Although anyone may commit to a vrata, most are made by women. As has been stated, Shakti (feminine strength) is revered in India. Women are believed to be much stronger in character and resolution than men. They are given the responsibility of keeping the karmic balance of the household. The knowledge of most of the sacred traditions of home and family are passed down through

223

the women. Although men are often involved in household pujas, it is the women who conduct almost all of the many other rituals that take place throughout each year, including the vratas, fasts, and other ascetic observances. A primary purpose of most of these is to lessen the burden of the family's bad karma, its toxicity, and thereby improve the status quo.

A vrata is a personal choice that does not require the services of a priest, Brahmana or otherwise. The rituals have been handed down in Hindu households from mother to daughter and from mothers-in-law to daughters-in-law for centuries. They are conducted by every class and community, and in every region, although they vary in form and demand according to the individual traditions of each family. Their strictures may be severe, but the rituals nevertheless encourage a freedom of artistic expression in music, dance, storytelling and poetry, artistry and craftsmanship.[5]

During the Chhattha Festival in Bihar, celebrated twice each year in February–March and October–November, women make vows to the Sun God, Surya, that if the condition of family members is improved (perhaps a disabled child will be healed or a long-unemployed husband will get a job), they will undertake annual fasts, intense prayers, and physical ordeals. The honoring of such a vrata may require days or even weeks of intense preparation. After dark on the evening before the festival day, a votary in a typical situation will create a temporary shrine of sugarcane

PATNA, BIHAR

The flames of lamps illuminate the sides and back of a terracotta elephant placed in a temporary shrine of sugarcane stalks inside the courtyard of an urban home. Behind the shrine a woman arranges offerings to the Sun God, Surya, as part of her rituals to fulfill a vow for the health of a family member.

stalks in the courtyard of her home. Beneath it she will place a terracotta elephant, representing a gift of honor to the God. Around the sculpture she arranges baskets of offerings: coconuts, fruit, special leaves, cooked sweets, incense, and rice. On the back of the elephant are small lamps that she fills with ghee and then lights. She will then pray to Surya, thanking him for his blessings. For the rest of the night until just before dawn, she and all the other women in her household will sing songs to Surya, praising him and relating stories of the many boons that he has granted his devotees. When the sky first begins to lighten, the family members will disassemble the shrine and carry the sugarcane, elephant, and all the baskets of offerings to the river. There they set up the shrine in the shallow waters near the riverbank, with the lighted elephant partially submerged. The woman who has made the vow will enter the river to her waist holding up the offerings to be blessed by the rising sun. Once her prayers are finished, she clambers ashore, and the food is divided to be eaten by all of the family members. Her actions are a means of showing her gratitude to Surya while at the same time contributing to the karmic balance of the entire family.[6]

An individual who has suffered a misfortune may decide to make a more exacting vow requiring an action that is particularly arduous and difficult to

perform. Such a vrata exemplifies the humility and deep respect of the devotee and should thereby bring a needed balance to negative karma and improve the situation. These vows will be made only in dire circumstances: as a part of prayers for healing an incurable disease or recovery from a personal or family disaster. For example, a farmer in Bihar might pray to Surya for the successful impregnation of his wife after years of impotence and infertility. He may vow that if his prayers are answered and his wife delivers a healthy son, he will perform the following humbling task during each annual Chhattha Festival for the next ten years. First he will stand outside his house with his hands folded in prayer and his heels touching the doorstep. Then he will prostrate himself on the ground, stretch his hands toward the river, pray, mark with his fingers the farthest point he can reach, stand again, and step to place his heels on that mark. He will then prostrate himself and repeat the process again and again—until he has reached the river's edge ten miles away. He will have planned so that he left the house at such a time to reach the river just at sunrise to make the appropriate puja to Surya on the day of Chhattha. The performance of this difficult vrata is considered to create such positive sacred energy in the devotee that other Hindus who pass him while he is prostrate will reach to touch the hem of his clothes, thereby having his darshan and gaining some of his merit for themselves. Vows of such intensity are not rare. Many devotees to Surya in Bihar, both men and women, may be observed enacting this same ritual during the Chhattha Festival.

PATNA, BIHAR

At an arduously slow pace, two men progress in prayer toward the Ganges River. At each step they prostrate themselves at full length upon the ground, repeat the name of the God Surya, then stand and pray before once again prostrating themselves.

Other demanding vratas elsewhere might include, for example, climbing on one's knees the two thousand steps to the temple of Amba Mata on Mount Girnar in Gujarat, or annually walking barefoot for four days up a jungle path to have darshan with the God Ayyappa in Sabarimala, Kerala, or making the painstaking pilgrimage to the 15,000-foot-high sacred lake at the base of Mount Kailasa, the legendary Himalayan abode of Shiva and Parvati.

Vows may include demonstrations of piety that require body piercing or fire walking. Some Hindus prepare with long periods of fasting and prayer, while for others the act may be spontaneous. In either case, the individual is usually overcome by trance, believing that he or she is imbued with the spirit of the deity. These devotees are compelled to show their intense devotion by, for example, piercing the tongue with a metal trident, or the back and limbs with metal spikes. Bleeding is rare: blood is a sign of impure faith. When the intrusive objects are removed, there is often no wound, no sign of a puncture. Similarly, worshippers, particularly in southern India, may vow to demonstrate their abiding faith by walking barefoot across a bed of red-hot coals. Those few that are burnt by this action are considered inappropriately prepared and not graced by the deity's spirit.[7]

Possession by a deity is not uncommon in India. Many festivals include members of the community who regularly become possessed to dance erratically through the crowds and to speak as oracles, giving direct messages to individuals, deciding disputes, and dispensing justice. However, this intensity of belief does not necessarily exemplify zealotry. A mainstream Hindu, conservative or liberal, from any walk of life (farmer or professor, princess or sweeper, rich or poor) may be possessed by a deity. Although this condition does not affect every Hindu, almost all families can recall at least one member who has been overcome by a spiritual trance. A trance may occur in the middle of a puja or while singing bhajanas (devotional hymns) or in having darshan with a deity during its procession on the street. The time and place are unpredictable. Typically, the devotee is overcome by a trance and begins to shake or roll on the ground or dance uncontrollably. He or she may mumble incoherently or cry out the name of the deity again and again or deliver divine messages, often very wise, in an unaccustomed voice. The trance may last minutes or hours or even days. When it is over, the person is often exhausted but elated. People who are possessed usually claim great insights and deep inner peace. Those who witness this transformation feel that they are in the presence of the Divine and that their lives are enhanced by the experience.

MANARASHALA, ALAPPUZHA
DISTRICT, KERALA

A devotee who is possessed by the spirit of the God Subramaniam is encircled by close friends who keep him from falling while he dances in oblivion. This experience is for him the fulfillment of a vow, something that he must undertake only once during his life.

In some cases, possession by a deity may be a planned and anticipated act, part of the fulfillment of a vow. Women may make vows to the Goddess Mariamman to be possessed by her spirit during her annual festival. Similarly, devotees of Subramaniam (also known as Murugan, Skanda, or Kartikeya, the son of Shiva and Parvati and brother of Ganesha) may vow that in return for a specific request (healing or the improvement of an oppressive situation), they will become possessed by the God at least once during their lives. If the wish is granted, the devotee will honor his part of the bargain during one of Subramaniam's three annual festivals, either in the following year or in any year thereafter. Some may wait decades before fulfilling their vows.

During one such festival a group of votaries assembles at a specified spot three miles from a temple dedicated to Subramaniam. Among them is a dentist, a farmer, a computer salesman, a shopkeeper, and a fisherman. Each votary brings a *kavadi*, a small domed palanquin made of sticks and brightly colored paper. The kavadi, symbolizing the legendary mountain of sins that the God carries on his shoulders on behalf of mankind, is placed with those of other devotees in the center of a sanctified area. Brahmana priests then conduct a puja to Subramaniam and purification rites on behalf of the devotees, tying vessels of water and offerings of food and flowers to the edges of each kavadi.

Aside from prayers and mental readiness, the only preparation that the votary makes is to take no solid food from early morning. No mind-altering drugs are employed. Once these first rituals are finished, the chief Brahmana rings a bell to signify readiness. The devotees then loudly call out the name of the God as they line up before the priest. The first man bows before him, touching the priest's feet and taking from him the newly blessed kavadi and a bunch of peacock feathers. At the moment he receives these two objects, he staggers back in trance, possessed by the God. His friends surge forward to catch him before he falls and to guide him away from the line of other devotees. As they leave, another votary approaches the priest, bows to receive his kavadi and feathers, and collapses in trance to be supported by friends. And then the next and the next until the entire group of votaries is in trance. Each votary is surrounded by a tight ring of close friends who hold hands around him throughout the period of possession. They make sure that he does not fall as he dances completely unaware of his surroundings. The votary, his friends, family, and observers all believe that he is possessed by the energy of the God Subramaniam. For the next several hours he dances while carrying the kavadi and peacock feathers as the entire group moves three miles in slow procession to the God's temple. Spectators believe that having darshan with these devotees is meritorious. When the parade of the possessed finally reaches the temple, they dance through the compound and into the sanctum. Once there, a final puja is made to Subramaniam and the deity is asked to leave his human vehicles and to once more inhabit the central image. The vow is complete, the votaries blessed with vibrant sacred energy, and all return to their homes.

MANARASHALA, ALAPPUZHA
DISTRICT, KERALA

Possession by a deity is a profoundly transformative experience. Not only is the devotee changed by his or her trance, but others who witness the possession often claim deep spiritual epiphanies.

Relationships with the Divine in India are believed to be reciprocal. By giving, you receive; and when receiving, it is essential that you acknowledge the source and give something in return. Health and good fortune are the natural products of a symbiotic relationship with the Gods. Misfortune and calamity are the result of imbalance, of inappropriate behavior and misguided thoughts and actions. Balance is regained through good deeds, proper conduct, abiding faith, and the appropriate honoring of one's deities. Occasionally a devotee might be required to conduct intense rituals to demonstrate devotion and to reestablish the karmic equilibrium. In this process, miracles are viewed as common occurrences, blessings bestowed by the Gods upon faithful devotees.

# The Final Stages:
# Old Age and Renunciation

NINE

The wise call him learned whose actions are all devoid of plans and desires for results." Dadaji repeats this verse in Sanskrit again and again, over and over and over to himself. In his right hand he holds his *mala*, his prayer beads made of sacred *rudraksha* seeds. He uses them to count the times he says this phrase from the Holy Gita, the words of God. Each time he reaches the last bead, the 108th, he begins again. Today he will stop when he has gone through the beads 108 times, after the 11,664th repetition of the phrase. This is his life these days, this is his entire duty. In it, he finds great peace.

It was not always so. Dadaji spent most of his life as a lawyer in a small city in central India. His attention was always focused on trying to win this action or that plea. He had worked from early morning, when he met his clients in the office in the front room of his house, through the long day in the civil courts, until late at night, when he finished preparing for the next day's litigations. Often it seemed that he hardly had time for his family: he was so wrapped up in his professional life and in trying to make enough money to support them. After all, besides his son's education, he had to provide the large dowries that his position demanded so that his two daughters might marry. It was not until four years ago, when he had just turned sixty-nine, that all the loans were paid off. Finally his duties were finished. His son, Bhupin, had passed through university and law school with highest marks. Bhupin was a lawyer himself now. He had married well and had three sons of his own to raise. Dadaji's two daughters were also content in their distant homes. Among these three progeny, he now had eight grandchildren. It was time to let it all go.

Dadaji had made the decision common to many elderly Hindus to leave his life of action and spend his remaining years in prayer and devotion. His wife, Avvaji, is alive and well. They have had a good life together, had few quarrels, and their relationship has grown strong and warmly affectionate through all the many hardships. Now Avvaji usually stays at home with the grandchildren, although sometimes she travels to visit their daughters' families. Occasionally she and Dadaji go on a pilgrimage together, down to the temples of southern India or up to the sacred sites in the mountains. But nowadays they are often apart. Dadaji is away from home most of the time—like this year, when he has come to Prayag to pray.

He is spending January through April camping in a small canvas tent alongside one of the most sacred spots in the world, the confluence of the Ganges and Jumuna Rivers. Two million other devotees are camped with him, a whole city of tents pitched in neat rows. Everyone is here for the same purpose: to bathe in the waters of the sacred rivers every morning, to meditate, to pray, and to attend the many religious discourses that continuously take place. Whole families attend—sometimes entire villages arrive together—as well as the massed followers of a particular guru and large groups of ascetics, and many, many retired people like himself.

Last year Dadaji had spent the same four months at the Kumbh Mela, the immense religious fair in Haridwar near the mouth of the Ganges. There, 20 million people had camped alongside the river to bathe and pray. The sense of vibrant spirit had been almost overwhelming then, but the Kumbh Mela takes place only every three years, alternating each time among four sacred spots. Because of its immense popularity, these smaller fairs had recently begun to take place, such as this Magh Mela at Prayag.

Dadaji shares his tent with two other elderly men: one had been an accountant, the other a pharmacist. Together they rise before dawn and walk out to the point of land closest to the confluence to dip in the chilly river, wash themselves, their dhotis and shawls, and then shiveringly pray to the sun just as it rises over the far bank. Then they return to their tent, make a quick cup of tea over the kerosene campstove, eat a few biscuits, and sit cross-legged in front of their tent to begin their daily rituals. Dadaji hasn't moved from his spot all day long. He is reading the *Bhagavad Gita*, the words of Krishna, one of the most sacred of all Hindu texts. It is a long process, in which he repeats just one verse again and again each day and meditates on its meaning. Tonight, like every other evening, he will join the other two to visit the meeting tent of a learned guru who will discourse in depth on the hidden messages in the Lord's words. There they will be fed their one true meal of the day: rice, lentils, a small portion of vegetables, and a couple of *chapattis* (unleavened bread). Long after dark they will return to their tent. Dadaji will chant a few evening prayers and stretch out on the thin reed mat that serves for his bed, curling himself in his blanket. It is a simple existence, so far from his home, but it agrees with him.

When he is distracted, he thinks about his family, about his children when they were growing up, about his relationship with Avvaji, about some of his court cases, the ones he was proud of and the ones he was unsure of, and about his favorite little grandson, who always climbs onto his lap as soon as he reaches home. But whenever he catches himself reminiscing he takes a deep breath and composes himself, saying more firmly the phrase that he is absorbing into his very being: "The wise call him learned whose actions are all devoid of plans and desires for results."[1] This is his duty now, this is his life: immersed so deeply in the words of God that he is transformed. He is becoming his faith.

Classical Hinduism divides human life into four ideal stages. The first two are integrally involved with society: the child and student who is still learning the fundaments of existence; and the householder who marries, works, and raises a family. The second two are concerned with removal from society: the elderly person whose responsibilities toward employment and family are finished and who may spend the remaining years in pursuit of spiritual goals; and the renunciate who chooses to reject all material possessions and familial bonds to live as an ascetic and mendicant.[2]

Many Hindus remain actively employed until they are very aged. The choice to retire, like every other, is circumstantial and individual. In the extended family household, the elderly are often indispensable. The matriarch or patriarch of a large family may be fully responsible for all decisions. Even when the elderly are not in control, their experience and wisdom are greatly respected. If they are retired from outside employment, they remain active in the household, preparing food, cleaning, and caring for their many grandchildren and great-nephews and -nieces. It is very rare for the elderly to be rejected by Indian families, as they often are by Western families. Close relationships between generations are still one of the foundations of Hindu society. The young, whose parents may be occupied with jobs away from the home, rely on their aged relatives to care for them and teach them. The knowledge of Hindu traditions and spirituality, still so essential in contemporary India, is largely maintained through this generational link.

Growing old is perceived as a blessing in India. It is a time of lessened responsibility and extended devotion. Many Hindus marry and have children at a young age. When they reach their seventies, they already may be great-grandparents. Their own children are assuming senior roles in the household, and even the simplest demands are no longer pressing. The majority of the rest of their lives may be spent in the reading of spiritual literature, in sacred discourse with both peers and juniors, and in meditation and prayer. These last years are a period for cleansing negative karma and preparing for death and eventual rebirth.

Many elderly individuals or couples go on pilgrimage either by themselves or with groups of devotees. They visit sacred sites throughout the country: temples, shrines, holy rivers or mountains, and the ashrams of revered gurus. Most of these places have facilities that provide shelter and sustenance to pilgrims, either free or at a nominal cost. Frequently a person will decide to stay in one

of these spots for weeks or months of prayer and meditation, like Dadaji in his tent in Prayag. Living in close proximity to and having regular darshan with a particularly holy image or saint is considered meritorious, bringing with it a pervading sense of peace and an influx of good karma. Most of these travelers keep in some sort of contact with their families, returning home for special holidays or to partake in samskara rituals. When they arrive, they may be viewed by the family with a certain awe. They bring with them the special energy gained by the intensity of their devotions. They provide a vital link to the broader diversity of Hindu beliefs, to a deeper knowledge of the common bonds of this ancient religion.[3]

Certainly the ability to afford pilgrimages is to a degree regulated by income. The destitute would be less likely to be able to travel. Even those who can make the choice may decide to remain at home. In most cases they will be respected for their need for solitude and left alone to conduct their prayers. Those that are literate may read and reread the ancient epics or the many treatises on religion or the books of prayer to their chosen deities. Some may write on slips of paper the name of a deity again and again, hundreds of thousands of times, as a means of quieting their minds and reaching out to the Divine. Others may practice one of the many forms of yoga or immerse themselves in the continuous repetition of a simple prayer or mantra. Each path is equally valid, each a means of letting go and preparing for the next transition.

VARANASI, UTTAR PRADESH

For more than fifty years this man, known as Homi Baba, has kept his vow to utter no sounds. He lives in complete silence, praying in a small shrine on the banks of the Ganges River. Many locals come to have his darshan and to gain tranquility by sitting in his presence.

## ASCETICISM

Within the fabric of Hindu society is the means for its rejection, for total escape from the boundaries of normal existence. Individuals who are so inclined are encouraged to step outside all convention, to live as hermits and ascetics and spend their years immersed in spiritual pursuits. The respected renunciation of community and property has been an integral part of Indian culture for thousands of years. While early Greek travelers described them as "naked philosophers," and later Westerners learned of them as "fakirs," the true name is Sadhu or Sannyasi (the latter refers to one who has been initiated by a guru into a specific mendicant order). The fourth stage, the act of complete renunciation, is very difficult. It means the total denial of all attachments: family, home, childhood friends, occupation, and possessions. All sensual pleasures are rejected: Sadhus and Sannyasis are celibate. They undertake vows of poverty and, for some, nudity, although most wear a minimum of clothes. Their lives are usually arduous: most do not stay in one place for more than three days.

They walk the long roads barefoot, oblivious to the biting cold of winter, the scorching heat of summer, and the torrential monsoon rains. They live outside or in whatever shelter is available to them, and they depend on donations for food. Many beg for their sustenance. As Hindu tradition extols giving alms to the needy, begging in India is considered an honorable profession.

More than 5 million Sadhus and Sannyasis live in India. The God Shiva is described as the first and the supreme ascetic: he renounced society to sit in silent meditation upon a mountaintop for millions of years, celibate and naked, his hair matted. The ascetic worshippers of Shiva and those of Vishnu are divided into two primary divisions. Most belong to one of ten specific mendicant orders first formed in the eighth century by the great Hindu saint Shankaracharya;[4] others are members of one of the sects that have been more recently established. The ideals and goals of these many Sadhus and Sannyasis vary greatly, from those who live as hermits in the mountains, entirely nude and covered with ashes, to those who live relatively well in large monasteries. Some are the yogis whose physical contortions and feats of self-denial are legendary throughout the world. A few follow the "left-hand path" of reverse behavior, sleeping on cremation grounds and drinking only from vessels made from human skulls. Whatever their choice, most are purely devout individuals whose sole aim is the lifelong pursuit of purification and the consequent removal of all past karma. With this complete cleansing, they hope to attain *moksha*, the release from rebirth and the reabsorption into the Absolute, Brahman.

They come from every walk of life. Some are raised as ascetics, given into the order as children. Others leave home in their teens, or as young men or women. Many choose to quit their jobs and leave their families in the midst of productive lives, feeling the undeniable call to asceticism and complete devotion to spirituality. It is not uncommon in India to meet a filthy, ash-covered Sadhu with matted dreadlocks and a long beard, clad only in a loincloth, and then discover that he was previously an engineer or a doctor, a train conductor or a teacher. Ninety percent of these ascetics are male. Orders of Sadvis (female renunciates) exist but are not as common. Hindus claim that women have much stronger ties to the home and to family responsibilities. Almost all of these Sadvis are widows whose choices by staying in the home were extremely limited. In renouncing the bonds of relationship and shelter, they endure hardships as ascetics that still allow them a freedom of action and expression of thought that would be impossible had they remained locked into the strictures of widowhood.

VARANASI, UTTAR PRADESH

An elderly Sadvi (a female renunciate) stops along the street to squat and whisper her affection into the ear of a tethered cow. In her left hand is a trishula (trident), which marks her as a member of a Sadvi sect of Shiva.

SANGAM, ALLAHABAD, UTTAR PRADESH

These two Sannyasis (male renunciates) spend several months each year caring for the many dressed images in this temporary shrine to Vishnu (shown in several of his incarnations). They conduct pujas on behalf of devotees as well as give instruction in yoga.

Many Sadhus and Sannyasis undertake remarkably demanding vows of self-denial and bodily torture as proof of their deep dedication to the Divine. They believe that these physical trials demonstrate their extraordinary piety and humility. The choice is individual. One Sadhu may vow never to utter a sound for the next twenty years. Another might decide that he will remain standing for twelve years, while another may vow to keep his arm straight and pointed to the sky for eight years. Still another may remain buried with only his head exposed for months at a time. By this enormous sacrifice of personal comfort, the devotee proves his deep faith in his deity, thereby removing his karmic imbalance and preparing himself for moksha.

Although virtually every ascetic lives in self-denial, not everyone undergoes such stringent vows of self-torture. Many practice rigorous yoga exercises intended to remove physical desires by linking the individual directly to the Divine within. Whatever his or her choices, the primary focus of all Hindu ascetics is honoring the sacred. Some believe in the formless unmanifest Brahman. Their means of contacting God may be primarily through sound: sacred words or mantras. Most maintain the beliefs of mainstream Hinduism in a Divine that is most accessible through images and primary elements such as fire and water. The major activity of the Sannyasis is to conduct regular pujas to their deities, rituals similar to those of householders and temple priests. Many Hindus believe that ascetics are in special contact with the Gods. It is considered particularly auspicious to be present at one of these pujas and to have darshan not only with the image but with the ascetic as a direct representative of the Divine.

**THANJAVUR, TAMIL NADU**

Many Sadhus perform feats of extreme physical self-denial or bodily mutilation to prove that their faith transcends material comfort. This itinerant renunciate has pierced his tongue with a trishula, a primary symbol of Shiva, to declare his dedication to and abiding faith in the God.

Traditionally, the only possessions allowed to a Sadhu or Sannyasi were his cotton loincloth and shawl, his begging bowl, his staff and prayer beads, and the symbols of his deity (the trident for Shiva or the conch for Vishnu). Although modernism has not touched these orders as much as it has contemporary Indian society, some changes have occurred. Eyeglasses and watches are worn by many, while some carry radios, cassette decks, or even CD players. It is not uncommon when traveling by bus or train in India to be accompanied by one or more ascetics, their tickets purchased by their many admirers. Some of the greatest gurus known in the West, such as Maharishi Mahesh Yogi, the disseminator of Transcendental Meditation, are Sannyasis—although their lifestyles might be viewed by many as less than ascetic. Hinduism accepts all paths to God.[5]

The ultimate goal of many ascetics, as it is for many mainstream Hindus, is to die in Varanasi, the most sacred Hindu city. Legend states that Varanasi was founded by Shiva eons ago. Many scholars believe that it is the oldest continuously lived in city in the world. It rises from the banks of that holiest of rivers, the Ganges, the Goddess incarnate. Within its precincts are tens of thousands of temples and shrines. Hindus believe that just to live in Varanasi is to worship God. They say that every action made there is sacred, every word a prayer. Millions of pilgrims come to Varanasi every year to the blessed waters of the Ganges. Just a sip of this water is believed to remove years of bad karma. To bathe in it is to cleanse oneself of lifetimes of wrongdoings. Hindu sages have stated that to die in Varanasi results in immediate moksha: complete freedom from reincarnation. The divine energy that permeates the city is so intense that, as one dies, the entire slate of past karma is wiped clean. The individual soul is absorbed into cosmic consciousness, into the all-consuming Absolute Brahman, never to be born again.[6]

VARANASI, UTTAR PRADESH

Each year the very elderly come to Varanasi to die, sometimes thousands arriving every day. They come to bathe in the river and to pray to the rising sun, to conduct their last pujas, to share in the pleasures of final darshan with their favorite deities. And they wait for death alongside temples and in the many hospices. When they have died, their bodies are ritually cremated and their ashes spread in the river to become one with the Goddess. For most, the choice is joyous. They are filled with a sense of deep peace. They are about to be fully released from all responsibility. All of the many rituals of this life and all their previous lives have been aimed toward this goal: they are becoming one with God and with all existence. No longer will they experience the toils or the joys of individual life. Now they will be a part of everything and they will be Divine: the complete complement of all opposites, of masculine and feminine, of dark and light, of good and evil. Their souls will permeate the universe to meet and finally become God.

This old man's only possessions are the clothes on his back, his books of sacred verses, and his few accoutrements of prayer. He has left behind family, friends, and all attachments to spend his last years in this most sacred city, purifying and preparing himself for *moksha*: release of his soul from the cycles of rebirth.

why isn't not ditching your family part of dharma?

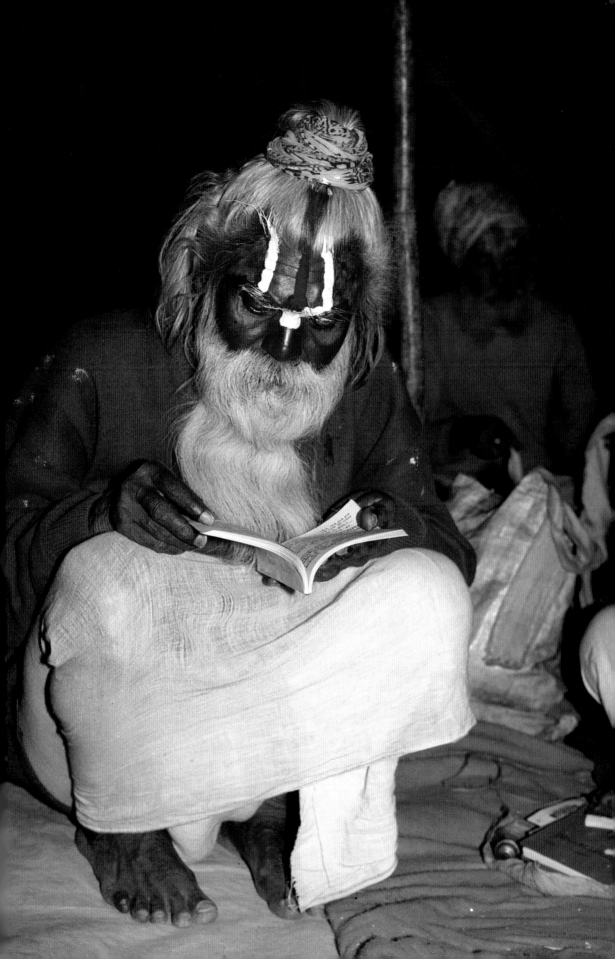

## CHAPTER ONE

**1** Many complex issues have been simplified here in order to present the underlying concepts of Hinduism as a basis for understanding the everyday rituals of India. Discussions about the nature of the Divine have divided Hindu philosophers for thousands of years. Innumerable books are devoted to deliberating the merits of monism, dualism, and pluralism. Many Hindus believe in a synthesis of the one and the many: an absolute indivisible power that coexists with many personalized Divine identities.

**2** The forty-three volumes of the Anthropological Survey of India are still being published, although many of the preliminary statistics are already available. The survey was conducted by five hundred scholars and twenty-six institutions from 1985–92 with interviews of 21,536 people in 4,513 villages and 941 towns. Much of the information is surprising and is causing major revisions of governmental and academic attitudes.

**3** In the last decade of the twentieth century Indian politics have been strongly influenced by new Hindu fundamentalist parties, such as the Bharatiya Janata Party (BJP). Members of these parties advocate conservative Hindu ideologies often directly opposed to the attitudes of liberals and non-Hindu minorities. Some critics state that the proposed return to traditional Hindu values ignores the underlying and pervasive Hindu concept of tolerance for individuals and other belief systems.

**4** Hinduism is sometimes divided into six primary sects: the three listed in the text and the followers of Surya, the Sun God, Ganesha (or Ganapati), the elephant-headed Remover of Obstacles, and Subramaniam (also known as Kartikeya or Skanda), the God of War. Each of these last three sects is considerably smaller than those of Shiva, Vishnu, and Shakti and are discussed briefly elsewhere in this book.

**5** The concept of Shakti is researched in detail through its manifestation in two Hindu societies, first in Wadley, *Shakti*, and second in Egnor, "On the Meaning of *Shakti* to Women in Tamil Nadu," in Wadley, *Powers of Tamil Women*.

**6** For detailed insight into the meaning of darshan and the personification of the Divine, see Eck, *Darshan*.

**7** Contemporary scholars are actively debating the assumption that the *Vedas* were compiled by early Aryan invaders into India in the mid-second millennium B.C.E. The new theories suggest that the previous belief was devised by Western classicists maintaining occidental and biblical primacy of advanced civilizations. Speculation based on a comparison of numerous archaeological, geological, astronomical, and philological factors suggests that the first *Veda* was compiled in approximately 4000 B.C.E., some 2,500 years earlier than previously assumed. Feuerstein, Kak, and Frawley, *In Search of the Cradle of Civilization*.

**8** Dozens of volumes are devoted to each of these primary Hindu texts. Although they are pertinent to innumerable contemporary Hindu rituals, the scope of this book does not permit more detailed descriptions of their contents.

**9** A more complete understanding of karma and dharma may be found in the *Bhagavadgita 3: Karma Yoga*; as well as O'Flaherty, *Karma and Rebirth*.

**10** An insightful discussion of the caste system may be found in Mandelbaum, *Society in India*, vols. 1 and 2.

**11** The term *Brahmana* in this book refers to the caste (varna), while the term *Brahman* refers to the undifferentiated Absolute Divine. In Indian languages the two words are written and pronounced identically. The common anglicization of the caste name to *Brahmin* is an incorrect spelling by Hindu standards.

## CHAPTER TWO

**1** Most strict Hindu rituals require the observance of sixteen upacharas in each puja. The form and method vary according to tradition. Most upacharas include the invocation and installation of the deity; the offering of water to the feet, head, and body of the image; bathing, dressing, perfuming, and adorning the image; burning incense; waving an oil lamp; offering food; prostration in front of the image; circumambulation; and leave-taking from the deity.

**2** The genesis for this book came from the exhibition entitled *Puja: Expression of Hindu Devotion*, held at the Smithsonian Institution's Arthur M. Sackler Gallery in Washington, D.C., co-curated by the author. In this exhibition Hindu images were displayed for the first time in an American museum as they were meant to be seen: bathed, dressed, adorned, and placed in shrines. The popularity of that exhibition has encouraged the creation of a traveling show of shrines and photographs with the same title as this book, intending to demonstrate the context and purpose of Hindu images and rituals of worship.

**3** Hundreds of books of Hindu sacred verses have been translated into English and other languages and are readily available in libraries and bookstores. A thorough understanding of Hinduism must include basic familiarity with these texts. Several are cited in the bibliography.

**4** A broad study of the pervasivness of reciprocity in Indian society is published in Nath, *Dana*.

**5** A detailed survey of the production and use of ritual terracottas as gifts for the Gods was published by the author: Huyler, *Gifts of Earth*.

**6** As elsewhere in this book, the details of the rituals described are generalizations drawn from pujas witnessed throughout India. As the practice of Hinduism is extremely individualistic, the forms that pujas take vary everywhere. The elements of Hindu rituals and their deeper significance are thoroughly discussed in Fuller, *Camphor Flame*.

**7** Esoteric teachings from many religions throughout the world describe energy centers of the body identical to the *chakras*. Numerous books are devoted to the study of the *chakras*, and *chakra* meditation and healing form the basis of many New Age philosophies.

## CHAPTER THREE

**1** For fascinating insights into some of the effects of contemporary media and consumerism on Hindu traditions, see Babb and Wadley, *Media and the Transformation of Religion*.

**2** Ghosh, *Cooking for the Gods*, gives detailed examples of some of the many rituals performed to create household balance in one eastern Indian state.

**3** Many good essays on the position and sacred roles of Hindu women may be found in Leslie, *Roles and Rituals for Hindu Women*. Also see Uberoi, *Family, Kinship, and Marriage in India*.

**4** Rituals are considered pivotal to maintaining equilibrium in Hindu households, and yet few scholarly treatises are devoted to them. Some notable exceptions are Sahai, *Hindu Marriage Samskara*, and Prasad, *The Sraddha*.

**5** For more comprehensive information about the worship and use of tulasi, see Huyler, *Gifts of Earth*, chap. 7.

**6** A broad survey of the ritual household decorations of Hindu women is contained in Huyler, *Painted Prayers*.

## CHAPTER FOUR

**1** See Nagaswamy, *Art and Culture of Tamil Nadu*, chap. 5.

**2** The seven most common names of these Saptamatrikas are Brahmi (the feminine of Brahma), Vaishnavi (the feminine of Vishnu), Maheshwari (the feminine of Shiva), Indrani (the feminine of Indra), Varahi (the feminine of Varaha, the boar incarnation of Vishnu), Kaumari (the feminine of Kumara, another name for Subramaniam, God of War), and Chamundi (the feminine power of Shiva as Shakti). In-depth scholarship about these seven Goddesses may be found in Misra, *Iconography of the Saptamatrikas*.

**3** An excellent survey of the rural shrines of gramadevatas throughout central India may be found in Maury, *Folk Origins of Indian Art*.

**4** For detailed information about the worship of Kali-Ma in eastern Uttar Pradesh, see Huyler, *Gifts of Earth*, chap. 6.

**5** A survey of votive terracottas in fourteen Indian states may be found in ibid., chap. 4.

## CHAPTER FIVE

**1** Brahmanism is discussed in detail in Biardeau, *Hinduism*, 17–40, 58–63.

**2** An interactive CD-ROM documenting the evolution and diversity of Hindu temples in North America was produced by a Harvard research team led by Diana Eck; it is entitled *On Common Ground: World Religions in America*.

**3** Dehejia, *Royal Patrons and Great Temple Art*.

**4** Kramrisch, *Hindu Temple*, vol. 1. Recent growth of both urban and rural communities has meant that not all temples can be placed on sites previously considered sacred. A site may be chosen simply because it is the only available land. Even in these situations, however, the rites of purification and the sacred positioning of shrines and their access is still considered of primary importance.

**5** The reasons for prohibiting non-Hindus from entering sacred areas are complex and difficult for the outsider to understand. They are derived in part from the belief, as discussed in Chapter 1, that human beings are responsible for all their actions—that even negative thoughts may create adverse reactions. Those not trained in the customs of approaching and honoring a sacred image might consciously or unconsciously pollute it. In the same way that the power of images and sacred spaces is believed to be enhanced by prayers and positive actions, it may also be damaged by careless or malevolent gestures, thoughts, or actions.

**6** An excellent introduction to the function and diversity of temples may be found in Michell, *Hindu Temple*.

**7** Dye, *Ways to Shiva*; Kramrisch, *Presence of Siva*; Meister, *Discourses on Siva*; and Subramuniyaswami, *Dancing with Siva*.

**8** According to Sunithi Narayan, "*Linga* means symbol and consists of three equal parts of the whole shaft. The part that is embedded in the ground is square and represents Brahma. The part that is enclosed by the circular receptacle is prismatic (either eight or sixteen-faced) and represents Vishnu. The last exposed part is cylindrical and represents Shiva.

All three together are the Linga, the connecting link between the abstract and material, the formless and the formed" (private correspondence).

**9** Mallebrein, "Masken der Gottheiten," in *Die Anderen Gotter*, 304–315.

**10** Dehejia, *Indian Art*, chap. 9.

**11** Ibid., 234–245.

**12** "Gold Images and Temple Jewellery from Madurai," in Nagaswamy, *Art and Culture of Tamil Nadu*, 115–119.

**13** Harman, *Sacred Marriage*.

**14** Hawley and Wulff, *Devi*; Hawley and Wulff, *Divine Consort*; and Kinsley, *Hindu Goddesses*.

**15** Harding, *Kali*.

**16** Rosen, *Vaisnavism*.

**17** Ranade, *Mysticism in India*.

## CHAPTER SIX

**1** Detailed descriptions of *mohras* (mask images) in worship in Himachal Pradesh may be found in Postel, Neven, and Mankodi, *Antiquities of Himachal*, chaps. 3 and 4.

**2** Many Hindu images in museums and private collections are damaged. Close inspection reveals broken fingers, a missing symbol, or a crack or chip in the stone or bronze. Because a damaged sculpture is no longer considered a divine receptacle, it may be viewed by the nonbeliever. The appearance of fully intact ancient sacred images in places where their divinity is not being appropriately honored is believed by some to be unethical. Hindu antipathy to contemporary attitudes of collecting and display has been exacerbated by the innumerable thefts of sacred objects, which have been subsequently smuggled out of India to be sold to collectors. Excellent research into the often opposing attitudes toward sacred Hindu objects in India and the West is found in Davis, *Lives of Indian Images*.

**3** See Pal, *Crafts and Craftsmen*; Shukla, *Vastu-Sastra: Hindu Canons of Iconography and Painting*; Kramrisch, *Hindu Temple*, vol. 2, chap. 8; and Vatsyayan, *The Square and the Circle*, chap. 6.

4 Swings are provided for the enjoyment of Gods and Goddesses in many regions of India. In many cases, such as the Dola Purnima Festival in Orissa, an image of the deity will be placed in a swing. Elsewhere in temple and household shrines images may permanently reside in swings, occasionally cast or carved as a single unit.

5 Occasionally wealthy devotees will lend their personal jewelry to adorn the image during a particular festival. By its direct contact with the "body" of the deity, this jewelry is believed to absorb great spiritual energy that will, in turn, benefit and empower its owner.

6 For a more thorough description of this festival, see Waghorne, "Dressing the Body of God."

7 Preston, "Creation of the Sacred Image," 12–22.

CHAPTER SEVEN

1 As recently as 1984, when writing *Village India*, I stated, "Nothing is wasted in India. Everything is used; every aspect of every object worked on, worked with, stretched to its limit, and made useful." Litter as it is known in the West is virtually nonexistent. All paper, plastic, rubber, and cloth was reused. The only rubbish was detritis and true garbage, and even that was used as compost. Foreign visitors complained of dirty streets and open sewers; but those conditions were caused by relative poverty and a dusty climate rather than wastage. Since the late 1980s an improving economy, a burgeoning middle class, and an influx of inexpensive synthetics have caused litter to be endemic, perhaps exacerbated by the increasing influence of Western attitudes through easily accessible satellite television. Now the streets of every town and city, and even those of many villages, are filled with litter. While previously anything that was thrown onto the street would be immediately picked up by someone to be reused, plastics are now so cheap and paper so available that people do not bother to recycle them.

2 See Bahadur, *Book of Festivals and Ceremonies*, chap. 4.

3 The creation of ephemeral sacred images, their use in shrines, and the rituals of their immersion are the primary focus of Huyler, *Gifts of Earth*.

4 Photographs of the production and use of these Chhattha images may be found in ibid., 99–102. Comparative descriptions of similar ephemeral images in the state of Orissa may be found in Preston, "Creation of the Sacred Image," 22–30.

5 More detailed photographs of this festival may be found in Huyler, *Gifts of Earth*, 102–107.

6 Bahadur, *Book of Festivals and Ceremonies*, chap. 20. In-depth research into the Goddess Durga and Durga Puja may be found in Kinsley, *Goddesses' Mirror*, chap. 1; Berkson, *Divine and Demonic*; and Coburn, *Devi Mahatmya*.

7 See Martin-Dubost, *Ganesa*; Grimes, *Ganapati*; Jagannathan and Krishna, *Ganesha*; and Subramuniyaswami, *Loving Ganesa*.

8 Preeminent research into the rituals of Ganesh Puja has been collated in Courtright, *Ganesa*.

CHAPTER EIGHT

1 An important study of the way that sacred elements affect health may be found in McGilvray, *Symbolic Heat*.

2 For an exhaustive probe of the basis of beliefs in traditional Indian healing, see Kakar, *Shamans, Mystics, and Doctors*.

3 See Ambalal, *Krishna as Srinathji*.

4 Karma is a difficult and complex concept to understand. For further study, see Fuller, *Camphor Flame*, 245–252.

5 More detailed information about vratas may be found in Susan S. Wadley, "Vratas: Transformers of Destiny," in Charles F. Keyes and E. Valentine Daniel, eds., *Karma: An Anthropological Inquiry* (Berkeley: University of California Press, 1983); and in Ray, *Ritual Art of the Bratas of Bengal*.

6 See Jayaswal and Krishna, *An Ethnoarchaeological View of Indian Terracottas*, 27–31. More complete photographs of the Chhattha Festival in Bihar are published in Huyler, *Gifts of Earth*, 80–83.

7 The sanskrit term used to describe the spirit behind these acts of faith is *tapas*, which may be translated as austerity, penance, or ascetic practice. It infers the special creative energy bestowed on a particularly faithful devotee that enables extraordinary actions. For the tapas experienced in particular by *Sadhus* (ascetics), see Hartsuiker, *Sadhus*, chap. 6.

CHAPTER NINE

1 Gambhirananda, *Bhagavadgita*, 4.19, p. 198.

2 Biardeau, *Hinduism*, chap. 2.

3 In-depth descriptions of Hindu pilgrimages and their meaning within society may be found in Bhardwaj, *Hindu Places of Pilgrimage*; and Gold, *Fruitful Journeys*.

4 Although early texts refer to mendicants and Sannyasis before the time of the great saint, Shankaracharya, it was his influence that first organized them into specific orders. The dates of this greatest of Hindu saints are disputed by scholars. Some believe that he lived in the seventh century, but most scholars state that it was in the eighth. Many books have been written about the Sadhus and Sannyasis, including the excellent Bedi, *Sadhus*; and Hartsuiker, *Sadhus*.

5 In the past several decades numerous people of non-Indian origin have joined Sannyasi orders, renouncing all their possessions and familial and cultural ties and undergoing arduous training to become wandering mendicants. One of the most famous of these, Agehananda Bharati (born Leopold Fischer) published a fascinating autobiography, *The Ocher Robe*.

6 A remarkable book about the sacred city of Varanasi (also known as Banaras and Kashi), including descriptions of many of its rituals, is Eck, *Banaras*. Through the microcosm of this one most important site, Eck gives perceptive insights into the broader practice of Hinduism.

# BIBLIOGRAPHY

## GENERAL HINDUISM

Bahadur, Om Lata. *The Book of Festivals and Ceremonies.* 2nd rev. ed. UBS Publishers' Distributors, New Delhi, 1997. ISBN: 81–7476–163–2.

Bhardwaj, Surinder Mohan. *Hindu Places of Pilgrimage in India: A Study in Cultural Geography.* University of California Press, Berkeley, 1983. ISBN: 0–520–04951–9.

Biardeau, Madeline. *Hinduism: The Anthropology of a Civilization.* Oxford University Press, New Delhi, 1997. ISBN: 0–19–563389–X.

Brockington, J. L. *The Sacred Thread: A Short History of Hinduism,* 2nd ed. Oxford University Press, New Delhi, 1997. ISBN: 0–19–564216–3.

Chakravarti, Sitansu S. *Hinduism: A Way of Life.* Motilal Banarsidass Publishers Private, Delhi, 1994. ISBN: 81–208–0899–1.

Chatterjee, Gautam. *Sacred Hindu Symbols.* Abhinav Publications, New Delhi, 1996. ISBN: 81–7017–320–5.

Cross, Stephen. *The Elements of Hinduism.* Element Books, Shaftesbury, Eng., 1994. ISBN: 1–86204–034–6.

Eck, Diana L. *Banaras: City of Light.* Routledge & Kegan Paul, London, 1983. ISBN: 0–7102–0236–9.

———. *Darshan: Seeing the Divine Image in India,* 2nd rev. and enlarged ed. Anima Books, Chambersburg, Pa., 1985. ISBN: 0–89012–042–0.

———. *Encountering God: A Spiritual Journey from Bozeman to Banaras.* Penguin Books, New Delhi, 1995. ISBN: 0–14–025533–8.

Feuerstein, Georg, Subhash Kak, and David Frawley. *In Search of the Cradle of Civlization.* Wheaton, Ill., 1995.

Fuller, C. J. *The Camphor Flame: Popular Hinduism and Society in India.* Princeton University Press, 1992. ISBN: 0–691–07404–6.

Gandhi, Mahatma. *What Is Hinduism?* Director, National Book Trust, New Delhi, India, 1994. ISBN: 81–237–0927–7.

Gold, Ann Grodzins. *Fruitful Journeys: The Ways of Rajasthani Pilgrims.* University of California Press, Berkeley, 1990. ISBN: 0–520–06959–5.

Housden, Roger. *Travels Through Sacred India.* Thorsons, London, 1996. ISBN: 1–85538–497–3.

Huyler, Stephen P. "Respecting Material Spirit," in *Asian Art* 5, no. 3 (Summer 1992): 2–7. Oxford University Press, New York. ISBN: 0–19–507534–X.

Kapur, Tribhuwan. *Religion and Ritual in Rural India: A Case Study in Kumaon.* Abhinav Publications, New Delhi, 1988. ISBN: 81–7017–238–1.

Knappert, Jan. *Indian Mythology: An Encyclopedia of Myth and Legend.* Aquarian Press, London, 1991. ISBN: 1–85538–040–4.

Kumar, Pramod. *Folk Icons and Rituals in Tribal Life.* Abhinav Publications, New Delhi, 1984.

Leslie, Julia, ed. *Roles and Rituals for Hindu Women.* Pinter Publishers, London, 1991. ISBN: 1–85567–299–5.

Maxwell, T. S. *The Gods of Asia: Image, Text, and Meaning.* Oxford University Press, New Delhi, 1997. ISBN: 0–19–563792–5.

McGilvray, Dennis B. *Symbolic Heat: Gender, Health and Worship Among the Tamils of South India and Sri Lanka.* Grantha Corp., Middletown, N.J., in association with University of Colorado Museum, Boulder, Colo., and Mapin Publishing, Ahmedabad, India, 1998. ISBN: 0–944142–87–7.

Narayan, Sunithi L., and Revathi Nagaswami. *Discover Sublime India: Handbook for Tourists.* Printed at Kartik Printers, Madras, India.

O'Flaherty, Wendy D., ed. *Karma and Rebirth in Classical Indian Traditions.* University of California Press, Berkeley, 1980.

Preston, James J. "Creation of the Sacred Image: Apotheosis and Destruction in Hinduism," in Joanne Punzo Waghorne and Norman Cutler, eds., in association with Vasudha Narayanan, *Gods of Flesh / Gods of Stone: The Embodiment of Divinity in India.* Anima Publications, Chambersburg, Pa., 1985. ISBN: 0–89012–024–2.

Raghavan, Dr. V. *Festivals, Sports and Pastimes of India.* B.J. Institute of Learning and Research, Ahmedabad, India, 1979.

Rosen, Steven J., ed. *Vaisnavism: Contemporary Scholars Discuss the Gaudiya Tradition.* Folk Books, New York, 1992.

Sharma, Brijendra Nath. *Festivals of India.* Abhinav Publications, New Delhi, 1978.

Shearer, Alistair. *The Hindu Vision: Forms of the Formless.* Thames and Hudson, London, 1993. ISBN: 0–500–81043–5.

Sontheimer, Gunther-Dietz, and Herman Kulke, eds. *Hinduism Reconsidered.* Manohar Publishers and Distributors, New Delhi, 1997. ISBN: 81–7304–198–9.

Stutley, Margret, and James Stutley. *A Dictionary of Hinduism: Its Mythology, Folklore and Development, 1500 B.C.–A.D. 1500.* Routledge & Kegan Paul, London, 1977. ISBN: 0–7100–8398–X.

Vedananda, Swami. *Aum Hindutvam: Daily Religious Rites of the Hindus.* Motilal Banarsidass Publishers, Delhi, 1993. ISBN: 81–208–1081–3.

Viswanathan, Ed. *Am I a Hindu? The Hindu Primer.* Halo Books, San Francisco, 1992. ISBN: 1–879904–06–3.

Waghorne, Joanne Punzo. "Dressing the Body of God," in *Asian Art* 5, no. 3 (Summer 1992): 8–33. Oxford University Press, New York. ISBN: 0–19–507534–X.

Waghorne, Joanne Punzo, and Norman Cutler, eds., in association with Vasudha Narayanan. *Gods of Flesh / Gods of Stone: The Embodiment of Divinity in India*. Anima Publications, Chambersburg, Pa., 1985. ISBN: 0–89012–024–2.

Walker, Benjamin. *Hindu World: An Encyclopedic Survey of Hinduism*, vols. 1 and 2. Indus, New Delhi, 1995. ISBN: 81–7223–179–2.

Werner, Karel. *A Popular Dictionary of Hinduism*. Curzon Press, Richmond, Eng., 1994. ISBN: 0–7007–0279–2.

Zaehner, R. C. *Hinduism*. Oxford University Press, London, 1972. ISBN: 0–19–500383–7.

## HINDU DEITIES

Ambalal, Amit. *Krishna as Shrinathji: Rajasthani Paintings from Nathdvara*. Mapin Publishing, New York, 1987.

Berkson, Carmel. *The Divine and Demonic: Mahisa's Heroic Struggle with Durga*. Oxford India Paperbacks, New Delhi, 1997. ISBN: 0–19–564371–2.

Chaturvedi, B. K. *Durga: Gods and Goddesses of India*: 7. Books For All, Delhi, 1996. ISBN: 81–7386–144–7.

Coburn, Thomas B. *Devi Mahatmya: The Crystallization of the Goddess Tradition*. Motilal Banarsidass Publishers, Delhi, 1997. ISBN: 81–208–0557–7.

Courtright, Paul B. *Ganesa: Lord of Obstacles, Lord of Beginnings*. Oxford University Press, New York, 1985. ISBN: 0–19–503572–0.

Danielou, Alain. *Hindu Polytheism*. Bollingen Foundation, New York, 1964. Library of Congress Catalog Card Number: 62–18191.

Dehejia, Vidya, ed. *The Legend of Rama: Artistic Visions*. Marg Publications, Bombay, 1994. ISBN: 81–85026–24–6.

Dye, Joseph M. *Ways to Shiva*. Philadelphia Museum of Art, 1980. ISBN: 0–87633–038–3.

Elliot, Julia, and David Elliott. *Gods of the Byways*. Museum of Modern Art, Oxford, 1982. ISBN: 0–905836–28–6.

Eschmann, Anncharlott, Hermann Kulke, and Gaya Charan Tripathi. *The Cult of Jagannath and the Regional Tradition of Orissa*. Manohar Publications, New Delhi, 1978.

Grimes, John A. *Ganapati: Song of the Self*. State University of New York Press, Albany, 1995. ISBN: 0–7914–2440–5.

Harding, Elizabeth U. *Kali: The Black Goddess of Dakshineswar*. Nicolas-Hays, York Beach, Maine, 1993. ISBN: 0–89254–025–7.

Harman, William P. *The Sacred Marriage of a Hindu Goddess*. Motilal Banardsidass Publishers, Delhi, 1992. ISBN: 81–208–0810–x.

Hawley, John Stratton, and Donna Marie Wulff, eds. *Devi: Goddesses of India*. University of California Press, Berkeley, 1996. ISBN: 0–520–20058–6.

———. *The Divine Consort: Radha and the Goddesses of India*. Beacon Press, Boston, 1982. ISBN: 0–8070–1303–x.

Jagannathan, Shakunthala, and Nanditha Krishna. *Ganesha: The Auspicious…The Beginning*. Vakils, Feffer & Simons, Bombay, 1995.

Jansen, Eva Rudy. *The Book of Hindu Imagery: The Gods and Their Symbols*. Binkey Kok Publications, Diever, Netherlands, 1997. ISBN: 90–74597–07–6.

Kinsley, David. *The Goddesses' Mirror: Visions of the Divine from East and West*. State University of New York Press, Albany, 1989. ISBN: 0–887706–836–7.

———. *Hindu Goddesses: Visions of the Divine Feminine in the Hindu Religious Tradition*. University of California Press, Berkeley, 1986. ISBN: 0–520–05393–1.

Kramrisch, Stella. *The Presence of Siva*. Princeton University Press, Princeton, N.J., 1981. ISBN: 0–691–10015–9.

Manna, Sibendu. *Mother Goddess Candi: Its Socio-Ritual Impact on the Folk Life*. Sankar Bhattacharya, Punthi Pustak International Booksellers & Publishers, Calcutta, 1993. ISBN: 81–85094–60–8.

Martin-Dubost, Paul. *Ganesa: The Enchanter of the Three Worlds*. Franco-Indian Research, Mumbai, 1997. ISBN: 81–900184–3-4.

Meister, Michael W., ed. *Discourses on Siva: Proceedings of a Symposium on the Nature of Religious Imagery*. Vakils, Feffer & Simon, Bombay, 1984. ISBN: 0–8122–7909–3.

Mitchell, A. G. *Hindu Gods and Goddesses*. Victoria and Albert Museum, London, 1982. ISBN: 0–11–290372–x.

O'Flaherty, Wendy Doniger. *Siva: The Erotic Ascetic*. Oxford University Press, London, 1973. ISBN: 0–19–520250–3.

Pintchman, Tracy. *The Rise of the Goddess in the Hindu Tradition*. State University of New York Press, Albany, 1994. ISBN: 0–7914–2111–2.

Saraswati, Swami Satyananda. *Chandi Path: She Who Tears Apart Thought*. Devi Mandir Publications and Motilal Banarsidass Publishers, Delhi, 1995. ISBN: 81–208–1307–3.

———. *Devi Gita*. Devi Mandir Publications and Motilal Banarsidass Publishers, Delhi, 1996. ISBN: 81–208–1386–3.

———. *Kali Puja*. Devi Mandir Publications and Motilal Banarsidass Publishers, 1997. ISBN: 81–208–1480–0.

Shulman, David Dean. *Tamil Temple Myths: Sacrifice and Divine Marriage in the South Indian Saiva Tradition*. Princeton University Press, Princeton, N.J., 1980.

Sontheimer, Gunther-Dietz. *Pastoral Deities in Western India*. Oxford University Press, New York, 1989. ISBN: 0–19–563293–1.

Subramuniyaswami, Satguru Sivaya. *Dancing with Siva: Hinduism's Contemporary Catechism*. Himalayan Academy, Kapaa, Hawaii, 1993. ISBN: 0–945497–47–4.

———. *Loving Ganesa: Hinduism's Endearing Elephant-Faced God*. Himalayan Academy, Kapaa, Hawaii, 1996. ISBN: 0–945497–64–4.

SACRED TEXTS

Chinmoy, Shri. *Commentaries on the Vedas, the Upanishads and the Bhagavad Gita: The Three Branches of India's Life-Tree*. Aum Publications, Jamaica, N.Y., 1996. ISBN: 0–88497–113–9.

de Bary, William Theodore. *Sources of Indian Tradition*, vol. 1. Columbia University Press, New York, 1958. ISBN: 0–231–08600–8.

Gambhirananda, Swami, trans. *Bhagavadgita*. Advaita Ashrama, Calcutta, 1995. ISBN: 81–7505–041–1.

Growse, F. S. *The Ramayana of Tulasidasa*. Motilal Banarsidass Publishers, Delhi, 1995. ISBN: 81–208–0205–5.

Mani, Vettam. *Puranic Encyclopaedia: A Comprehensive Dictionary with Special Reference to the Epic and Puranic Literature*. Motilal Banarsidass Publishers, Delhi, 1984. ISBN: 0–89581–172–3.

Panikkar, Raimundo. *The Vedic Experience: An Anthology of the Vedas for Modern Man and Contemporary Celebration*. Narendra Prakash Jain for Motilal Banarsidass Publishers, New Delhi, 1994. ISBN: 81–208–1280–2.

Radhakrishna, S., ed. *The Principal Upanisads*. Indus, New Delhi, 1996. ISBN: 81–7223–144–X.

Shukla, D. N. *Vastu-Sastra*. Vol. 1: *Hindu Science of Architecture*. Munshiram Manoharlal Publishers, New Delhi, 1993. ISBN: 81–215–0611–5.

———. *Vastu-Sastra*. Vol. 2: *Hindu Canons of Iconography and Painting*. Munshiram Manoharlal Publishers, New Delhi, 1993. ISBN: 81–215–0612–3.

Zimmer, Heinrich, with Joseph Campbell (ed.). *Philosophies of India*. Bollingen Foundation, New York, 1951.

ART HISTORY

Allchin, Bridget, ed. *Living Traditions: Studies in the Ethnoarchaeology of South Asia*. Oxford & IBH Publishing, New Delhi, 1994. ISBN: 81–204–0901–9.

Archana with Gita Narayanan, ed. *The Language of Symbols: A Project on South Indian Ritual Decorations of a Semi-Permanent Nature*. Crafts Council of India, New Delhi.

Babb, Lawrence A., and Susan S. Wadley. *Media and the Transformation of Religion in South Asia*. University of Pennsylvania Press, Philadelphia, 1995. ISBN: 0–8122–1547–8.

Blurton, T. Richard. *Hindu Art*. British Museum Press for the Trustees of the British Museum, London, 1992. ISBN: 0–7141–1442–1.

Davis, Richard. *Lives of Indian Images*. Princeton University Press, Princeton, N.J., 1997. ISBN: 0–691–02622–X.

Dehejia, Vidya. *Indian Art*. Phaidon Press, London, 1997. ISBN: 0–7148–3496–3.

Dehejia, Vidya, ed. *Royal Patrons and Great Temple Art*. Marg Publications, Bombay, 1988.

Devi, Pria, and Richard Kurin. *Aditi: The Living Arts of India*. Smithsonian Institution Press, Washington, D.C., 1985. ISBN: 0–87474–853–4.

Ghosh, Pika. *Cooking for the Gods: The Art of Home Ritual in Bengal*. Michael W. Meister, ed. Newark Museum, N.J., 1995. ISBN: 0–932828032–9.

Huntington, Susan L. *The Art of Ancient India: Buddhist, Hindu, Jain*. John Weatherhill, New York, 1985. ISBN: 0–8348–0183–3.

Huyler, Stephen P. *Gifts of Earth: Terracottas and Clay Sculptures of India*. Grantha Corp., Middletown, N.J., in association with Mapin Publishing, Ahmedabad, and Indira Gandhi National Centre for the Arts, New Delhi, 1996. ISBN: 0–944142–48–6.

———. *Painted Prayers: Women's Art in Village India*. Rizzoli International Publications, New York, 1994. ISBN: 0–8478–1809–8.

Jayaswal, Vidula, and Kalyan Krishna. *An Ethnoarchaeological View of Indian Terracottas: A Comparative Study of the Present and Past Terracotta Traditions of Gangetic Plains*. Agam Kala Prakashan, Delhi, 1986.

Kramrisch, Stella. *Manifestations of Shiva*. Philadelphia Museum of Art, 1981. ISBN: 0–87633–039–1.

———. *The Hindu Temple*, vols. 1 and 2. Motilal Banarsidass Indological Publishers & Booksellers, Delhi, 1976.

———. *Unknown India: Ritual Art in Tribe and Village*. Philadelphia Museum of Art, 1968. Library of Congress Catalog Card Number: 68–14542.

Kumar, Nita. *The Artisans of Banaras: Popular Culture and Identity, 1880–1986*. Princeton University Press, Princeton, N.J., 1988. ISBN: 0–691–05531–9.

Mallebrien, Cornelia. *Die Anderen Gotter: Volks- und Stammesbronzen aus Indien*. Rautenstrauch-Joest-Museum, Cologne, 1993. ISBN: 3–923158–25–4.

Maury, Curt. *Folk Origins of Indian Art*. Columbia University Press, New York, 1969. ISBN: 231–03198–x.

Meister, Michael W., ed. *Making Things in South Asia: The Role of Artists and Craftsman*. Proceedings of the South Asia Seminar 4 (1985–86): xvii–216, University of Pennsylvania, Philadelphia. ISBN: 0–936115–03–3.

Michell, George. *The Hindu Temple: An Introduction to Its Meaning and Forms*. University of Chicago Press, Chicago, 1988. ISBN: 0–226–53230–5.

Miller, Barbara Stoler, ed. *Exploring India's Sacred Art: Selected Writings of Stella Kramrisch*. University of Pennsylvania Press, Philadelphia, 1983. ISBN: 0–8122–1134–0.

Misra, O. P. *Iconography of the Saptamatrikas*. Agam Kala Prakashan, Delhi, 1989.

Mitter, Partha. *Much Maligned Monsters: History of European Reactions to Indian Art*. Oxford University Press, Oxford, 1977. ISBN: 0–19–817336–9.

Mookerjee, Ajit. *Ritual Art of India*. Thames and Hudson, New York, 1985. ISBN: 0–500–23423–x.

Murti, Vishnu. *Indian Art*. University Art Gallery, University of Massachusetts at Amherst, February–March 1974.

Nagaswamy, R. *The Art and Culture of Tamil Nadu*. Sundeep Prakashan, Delhi, 1980.

Nandagopal, Dr. Choodamani, and Vatsala Iyengar. *Temple Treasures*. Vol. 1: *Ritual Utensils*, and vol. 2: *Temple Jewellery*. Crafts Council of Karnataka, India, 1995.

Pal, M. K. *Crafts and Craftsmen in Traditional India*. Kanak Publications, New Delhi, 1978.

Postel, M., A. Neven, and K. Mankodi. *Antiquities of Himachal*. Franco-Indian Pharmaceuticals, Bombay, 1985.

Ray, Sudhansu Kumar. *Ritual Art of the Bratas of Bengal*. Firma K. L. Mukopadhyay, Calcutta, n.d.

Vatsyayan, Kapila. *The Square and the Circle of the Indian Arts*. Roli Books, New Deli, 1983.

SOCIAL BEHAVIOR

Bedi, Rajesh. *Sadhus: The Holy Men of India*. Brijbasi Printers, New Delhi, 1991. ISBN: 81–7101–021–3.

Bharati, Agehananda. *The Ocher Robe: An Autobiography*. Doubleday Anchor, New York, 1970.

Hartsuiker, Dolf. *Sadhus: India's Mystic Holy Men*. Inner Traditions International, Rochester, Vt., 1993. ISBN: 0–89281–454–3.

Humphrey, Caroline, and Stephen Hugh-Jones, eds. *Barter, Exchange, and Value: An Anthropological Approach*. Cambridge University Press, New York, 1992. ISBN: 0–521–40682–x.

Kakar, Sudhir. *Shamans, Mystics, and Doctors: A Psychological Inquiry into India and Its Healing Traditions*. Oxford India Paperbacks, 1992. ISBN: 0–19–562793–8.

Maloney, Clarence. *Peoples of South Asia*. Holt, Reinhart, and Winston, New York, 1974. ISBN: 0–03–084969–1.

Mandelbaum, David. *Society in India*. Vol. 1: *Continuity and Change*, and vol. 2: *Change and Continuity*. University of California Press, Berkeley, 1970. ISBNS: 0–520–01623–8 and 0–520–01895–8.

Nath, Vijay. *Dana: Gift System in Ancient India (c. 600 BC–c. AD 300): A Socio-Economic Perspective*. Munshiram Manoharlal Publishers, New Delhi, 1987. ISBN: 81–215–0054–0.

Prasad, R. C., trans. *The Sraddha: The Hindu Book of the Dead*. Motilal Banarsidass Publishers, Delhi, 1995. ISBN: 81–208–1192–5.

Raheja, Gloria Goodwin. *The Poison in the Gift: Ritual, Prestation, and the Dominant Caste in a North Indian Village*. University of Chicago Press, Chicago, 1988. ISBN: 0–226–70729–6.

Ranade, R. D. *Mysticism in India: The Poet Saints of Maharashtra*. State University of New York Press, Albany, 1983.

Sahai, Prem. *Hindu Marriage Samskara: Marriage Rites and Rituals of Hindus*. Wheeler Publishing, Allahabad, India, 1993. ISBN: 81–85814–12–0.

Uberoi, Patricia. *Family, Kinship, and Marriage in India*. Oxford University Press, New York, 1993. ISBN: 0–19–562835–7.

Wadley, Susan S., ed. *The Powers of Tamil Women*. Maxwell School of Citizenship and Public Affairs, Syracuse University, Syracuse, N.Y., 1980. ISBN: 0–915984–82.

———. *Shakti: Power in the Conceptual Structure of Karimpur Religion*. Department of Anthropology, University of Chicago, Chicago, 1975. ISBN: 0–916256–0–4.

**Agni** God of Fire

**Amma (Amman)** Mother; often refers to the Goddess

**Annapurna** the Goddess of Food

**arati** refers to both the tray that carries the flame used in worship and the flame itself

**Ardhanari** the supreme deity Shiva depicted as half man and half woman

**ashram** a place of physical retreat usually associated with a guru (great teacher)

**avatar** incarnation; usually refers to one of the incarnations of Vishnu

**Ayyanar** the southern Indian God who protects the boundaries of a community

**Balaji** Vishnu, also known as Sri Venkateshwara

**Bhagavad Gita (Gita)** one of the most sacred texts of Hinduism, describing the lessons given by Krishna to the great warrior Arjuna

**Bhagavati** one of the names of the Divine Feminine in her form as the Destroyer of Evil (Chamundi, Chandi, and Kali)

**bhajana** hymn, devotional song

**Bhakti** the form of Hinduism based on the supremacy of Divine Love

**Bhudevi** the Earth Goddess

**bindi** the dot placed in the center of a woman's forehead. Its derivation is religious, but for most women it is simply a statement of fashion.

**Brahman** the Absolute, Unmanifested, Supreme Deity

**Brahmana** (often elsewhere spelled Brahmin or Brahman) the priestly caste; one of the four primary varnas (castes) of Hindus

**chakras** the seven vortexes of energy that, according to Hindu mysticism, are manifest within the human body

**Chamundi (Chamunda)** one of the names of the Divine Feminine in her form as the Destroyer of Evil (Bhagavati, Chandi, and Kali)

**Chandi** one of the names of the Divine Feminine in her form as the Destroyer of Evil (Bhagavati, Chamundi, and Kali)

**Chatur Mukha Linga** the primary aniconic image of the God Shiva portrayed with four faces (chatur mukhas), each facing one of the cardinal directions

**Chhattha** a festival dedicated to the Sun God, Surya, celebrated twice each year in the eastern Gangetic Plain

**Dakshina Murti** the God Shiva in his form as the Divine Teacher

**dana** the act of giving

**darshan** literally translated as "seeing and being seen by God," referring to that moment when a devotee is blessed by personal contact with a deity, a highly revered person, or a sacred object

**deepa** a wick lamp fueled by oil or ghee

**devasthana** a community shrine

**Devi** a generic term for a Goddess

**dharma** Divine Law, righteousness, duty

**Divali** the Festival of Lights held in the lunar month of October–November to celebrate the reemergence of the sun after the long rainy season; also often associated with the worship of the Goddess Lakshmi

**Dola Purnima** the festival in which the image of a deity is placed in a swing

**Durga** the Goddess in her form as the Divine Warrior, often shown riding a tiger or lion

**Dussehra** the ten-day autumn festival honoring the Goddess Durga and her triumph over the demon king Mahisasura; also the celebration of the God Rama's destruction of the demon king Ravana and his rescue of his wife, Sita, from captivity

**Ganesha (Ganapati)** the elephant-headed God, Remover of Obstacles and Lord of Beginnings; son of Shiva and Parvati

**Ganesha Chaturthi** the ten-day festival celebrating Ganesha in the lunar month of August–September

**Ganga** the Ganges, the most sacred of Hindu rivers, viewed as a Goddess

**garba grha** literally translated as "womb," the sanctum sanctorum of a temple

**Gauri** the Goddess of Agricultural Abundance

**ghee** clarified butter

**gopuram** a towering gateway that marks the entrance to a southern Indian temple

**gramadevata** generic term for a deity of community

**guru** revered teacher

**Hanuman** the Monkey God, messenger of the Gods, particularly associated with worship of the God Rama; the epitome of devoted service and loyalty, he is honored in his own right for his great asceticism and learning

**Harijan** Mahatma Gandhi's word to describe those who live outside the caste system, previously referred to as "outcaste" or "untouchable"

**ishtadevata** one's personal, chosen deity

**Jagannath** a form of Vishnu worshipped in one of Hinduism's most sacred temples, in Puri, Orissa

**jati** subcaste

**Kailasa** the Himalayan mountain believed to contain the palace of Shiva and Parvati—for Shaivites comparable to the Greek Mount Olympus

**Kali** one of the names of the Divine Feminine in her form as the Destroyer of Evil (Bhagavati, Chandi, and Chamundi)

**Kali-Ma** a regional form of the great Goddess Kali, worshipped as a community deity in the north-central Gangetic Plain

**karma** translated literally as "action"; the law of cause and effect that states that every action and even every thought has consequences that will manifest themselves later

**karpura** camphor

**Kartikeya** (also known as Murugan, Skanda, or Subramanium) the Warrior God, hero son of Shiva and Parvati and brother to Ganesha

**kolam** a sacred design usually drawn by women upon the ground in front of a southern Indian house to protect the family's welfare

**Krishna** an incarnation (avatar) of Vishnu who was born in northern India as a cowherd and whose exploits during his life made him one of Hinduism's most beloved heroes; also the wise adviser whose discourses provide the basis for the epic *Mahabharata*

**Kshatriya** the caste of warriors and leaders; one of the four varnas, or primary castes

**kuladevata** the household or family deity

**Kumbh Mela** an enormous festival held once every twelve years in each of four sacred spots in India, moving to the next spot every three years

**kumkum** vermilion

**Lakshmi** Goddess of Abundance and Prosperity, wife of Vishnu; often shown associated with elephants and lotuses

**Linga** the aniconic image of Shiva most commonly found in worship in his temples; many scholarly treatises refer to its phallic form, but for most devout Hindus that reference is offensive

**Ma (Mata, Mataji)** Mother; often refers to the Goddess

**Mahabharata** the longest epic poem in the world and one of the primary Hindu epics that refers to the period before, during, and after the great war between the Pandavas and Kauravas; it lays the foundations for Hindu morality, duty, and the meaning of life, death, and salvation

**maharajah** king

**Mahashivaratri** the most important festival in honor of the great God Shiva, celebrated in the lunar month of February–March

**mala** garland

**Manasa** the Goddess of Snakes worshipped to prevent snakebite and as an aid in healing from poison

**mandala** a geometric diagram, often used in meditation

**mantra** sacred word or words repeated continually as a tool for meditation

**Mariamman** worshipped in southern India as the Goddess of Smallpox, the Provider of Good Fortune, and the Protector of Children

**Meenakshi** a southern Indian (Tamil) name for the Supreme Goddess Parvati, bride of Shiva (Sundareshwara)

**mohra** a processional deity personified by a mask, normally made of brass, silver, or gold, found only in the foothills of the western Himalayas

**moksha** release from rebirth through mergence with the Absolute, the cosmos

**Mukha Linga** the primary aniconic image of the God Shiva portrayed with a face

**Murugan** (also known as Skanda, Kartikeya, or Subramanium) the Warrior God, hero son of Shiva and Parvati and brother to Ganesha

**Naga** cobra; the worship of snakes and snake images for good health and fertility is particularly strong in eastern and southern India

**Nandi** the bull mount of Shiva, symbol of steadfast loyalty to the Gods

**Narasimha** the lion avatar (incarnation) of Vishnu

**Nataraja** Shiva in his form as the Cosmic Dancer

**Navaratri** the nine-day autumn festival celebrating the Goddess Durga

**Om** the most sacred mantra, considered by many to be the pure distillation of the universe into sound, transcendent and timeless

**padukas** the sandals of saintly beings worshipped in their stead

**Parabrahman** the supreme Godhead permeating all existence and unmanifested in any single form

**Parvati** the Supreme Goddess, the Divine Feminine, consort of Shiva; some of her other forms are known as Durga, Kali, and Gauri

**peepul** a sacred tree of the ficus (fig) family

**pinda** a small mound symbolic of the Goddess in north-central India

**pradakshina** ritual circumambulation of the sanctum of a temple

**Prajapati** the God of Creativity

**prana pratishtha** the ritual that breathes the life force into a sacred image of a deity

**prashad** offerings, usually referring to food, that have been blessed by a deity during puja and are returned to be distributed and eaten by the devotees

**puja** the sacred ceremonies of worship

**pujari** a priest or officiant of a puja

**Puranas** ancient sacred texts

**Rama** an avatar (incarnation) of Vishnu and hero of the epic *Ramayana* who epitomizes loyalty, bravery, strength, and responsibility; his relationship with his wife, Sita, epitomizes the perfect Hindu marriage

**Ramayana** one of Hinduism's most important epics, which, through the story of Rama and Sita, provides ethical paradigms for all aspects of life and relationships

**Ravana** the ten-headed demon who abducts Sita in the *Ramayana*

**rudraksha** the seed of the *rudraksha* tree (*Elaeocarpus ganitrus roxb.*), considered particularly sacred to Shiva. It is worn by his devotees either singly or on a string to be used as a rosary for counting prayers.

**Sadhu (fem. Sadvi)** an ascetic who has renounced the bonds of family and possession to devote his or her life to prayer and ritual

**salagrama** a fossilized ammonite symbolic of Vishnu

**samskara** the rituals that celebrate life-changing episodes, such as birth, coming of age, betrothal, and marriage

**Sanatana Dharma**  a term commonly used to refer to Hinduism

**Sannyasi**  an ascetic who has renounced the bonds of family and possession to devote his or her life to prayer and ritual and has been accepted by a specific teacher as a member of a mendicant order

**Sanskrit**  the sacred and literary language of ancient and medieval India that continues to be the primary vehicle for the transmission of sacred texts and the performance of sacred rituals

**Saptamatrikas**  the Seven Mother Goddesses worshipped throughout India as the guardians of community

**Saraswati**  the Goddess of Learning, the Arts, Music, and Dance, often shown holding a book, playing a *veena* (stringed instrument) and riding or accompanied by a swan

**sari**  the traditional garment of women in many parts of South Asia composed of a length of material, usually between five and six yards, that is wrapped around the body

**Shaiva**  a worshipper of Shiva and his associated family

**Shakti**  literally translated as "strength" and "power," Shakti also refers to the active Divine Feminine

**shikhara**  the tower that rises directly above the sanctum of a northern Indian temple

**Shiva**  God of Creation and Destruction; perfect blend of all opposites; considered by many Hindus to be the supreme deity; most often represented by a Linga; consort of the Goddess Parvati

**shlokas**  sacred verses, often in the form of prayers

**Shridevi**  the Goddess, Consort of Vishnu

**Shudra**  the caste of craftsmen and laborers; one of the four varnas, or primary castes

**Sita**  the wife of Rama, whose abduction by the demon Ravana and subsequent rescue by her husband provides the plot of the epic *Ramayana*

**Sitala**  worshipped in northern India as the Goddess of Smallpox, the Provider of Good Fortune, and the Protector of Children

**Skanda**  (also known as Kartikeya, Murugan, or Subramanium) the Warrior God, hero son of Shiva and Parvati and brother of Ganesha

**Sraddha**  the rituals associated with death

**Srinathji**  a name for Krishna (Vishnu)

**Subramaniam**  (also known as Kartikeya, Murugan, or Skanda) the Warrior God, hero son of Shiva and Parvati and brother of Ganesha

**Sundareshwara**  another name for Shiva

**Surya**  the Sun God; the source of all knowledge, according to Hindu mythology

**swyambhu**  self-created, its existence not dependent on the aid of any other being

**tapas**  the performance of a spiritual discipline; austerity, penance, or ascetic practice

**Thakurani**  (gramadevata) a generic term for the Goddess associated with and protecting individual communities in eastern India (Orissa)

**tilak**  a mark on the forehead of a devotee that signifies the object of his or her devotion

**trishula**  trident, symbol of Shiva and Shakti

**tulasi**  sacred basil (*Ocimum sanctum*), worshipped in India as the incarnation of the Goddess Lakshmi

**upacharas**  the individual ritual acts performed as preparation for and during pujas

**Upanishads**  ancient philosophical and mystical treatises that form much of the basis of Hindu esoteric thought

**utsava murti**  a processional image imbued with the potent energy of a deity for a specific period of time

**vahana**  the vehicle of a deity, usually an animal

**Vaishnava**  a worshipper of Vishnu and his associate family

**Vaishyas**  the caste of merchants and businessmen; one of the four varnas, or primary castes

**Varaha (Varahi)**  the boar avatar (incarnation) of Vishnu

**varna**  caste

***Vedas***  the primary and most ancient scriptures of Hinduism, recognized as divine revelation (*shruti*), and comprising four books of hymns: the *Rg. Veda*, the *Sama Veda*, the *Yajur Veda*, and the *Atharva Veda*

**Venkateshwara**  (also known as Balaji) one of the names of Vishnu, usually associated with his manifestation in Tirupati

**Venugopala**  Krishna (Vishnu) in his form as the flute-playing cowherd

**vibhuti**  sacred ash

**vimana**  the domed or towered building that contains the sanctum in a southern Indian temple

**Vishnu**  the Preserver, who sustains the universe and periodically incarnates on earth to assist the Gods or mankind in their need; considered by many Hindus to be the supreme deity; always associated with his consort, Lakshmi or Saraswati

**Vishvakarma**  the Progenitor, Creator of the Universe

**vrata**  a sacred vow

**yantra**  a sacred diagram

**yoga**  a regimen of self-discipline intended to open the mind and body to sacred energy

**yogi**  a practitioner of yoga

**Yoni**  the feminine principle; the holder or receptacle on which the Linga sits

# ACKNOWLEDGMENTS

I am grateful beyond words to the many thoughtful people who have helped me to open my mind and be receptive to learning about Hinduism.

I am the product of generations of deeply religious family members, many of whom exhibited tolerance of others and fascination with other cultures. I am particularly grateful to my parents, Margaret and Jack Huyler, my Uncle Coulter Huyler, both my grandmothers, and my Aunt Manie. Reginald and Gladys Laubin spent their lives recording and preserving Plains Indian ritual art and culture, and their influence on me as a young child cannot be overemphasized. I grew up in Ojai, California, a small town populated by many interested in India and eastern religions, including its most famous citizen, the Indian philosopher J. Krishnamurti. Since the age of eight I have benefited immeasurably from the friendship of Mme. Andree Schlemmer.

When I was just eighteen I was befriended by Beatrice Wood, an elderly artist and one of the founders of Dada. She invited me to travel to India with her the following year. Until her death last year, Beatrice remained a cornerstone of my life, a person who shared my passion for India and her cultures, and whose profound intellect and sense of ethics always inspired my own learning process. At the University of Denver, three fine scholars introduced me to my research: Charles Geddes, Kate Peck Kent, and Mary Lanius. I arrived in India on my twentieth birthday and, through Beatrice, was introduced to a wide circle of friends that became the foundation of a kinship to India that has lasted almost three decades. Shortly after my return from my first trip I married Helene Wheeler, the most important person in my life, whose undaunting support and love has underpinned everything that I have done since that time.

Throughout my career I have been helped to a deeper understanding of Hinduism by many: during my doctoral studies at the University of London by William Archer, John Marr, George Michell, Heather Elgood, and the work of C. J. Fuller; and in the United States by the work of Diana Eck, Joanna Waghorne, and John S. Hawley, among many others, and by the staff and writers for *Hinduism Today*. Perhaps the most important impetus to this work was the commission by Dr. Milo Beach, director of the Smithsonian's Freer and Sackler Galleries, to curate an exhibition on Hindu sacred art. Gathering information for that exhibition ("Puja: Expressions of Hindu Devotion") and synthesizing it into presentable form taught me immeasurably. The perception and brilliance of my co-curator, Sarah Ridley, of the Freer and Sackler's Education Department, were of invaluable aid. For their help in gathering and presenting material for "Puja" I am also grateful to the extended staff of the Freer and Sackler Galleries, to Paul Walter, to Maharukh Desai, to many fellow scholar-members of the American Committee for Southern Asian Art, and to Uma Nagarajan and the priests and staff of the Shiva-Vishnu Temple in Lanham, Maryland.

As most of my time is spent in the field conducting research or writing, I rarely have the chance to teach extensive courses. In 1996, I was given the opportunity by Ohio State University's department of art history to teach a graduate class in Hindu ritual. The preparation for that course and the perceptive responses of my students taught me a great deal that has been incorporated into this book. I have led many academic tours to India. The members of my three last tours have been of particular aid to me in gathering material for this book: the Painted Prayers Tour (1995), the Magic Carpet Tour (1997) and the Sackler Docent Puja Tour (1998). The members are too numerous to thank individually, but they should know that I am grateful to each of them for the insights they provided by their questions and viewpoints. During the writing of this book I have received invaluable feedback and suggestions from Karen Lukas, Barbara Goodbody, Nora Fisher, Elizabeth Baldwin, Becca Swan, Lyn Donovan, Paula Clough, Leslie Panton, and Sara Foltz, and the loving support of my good friends in my men's group. The constant presence of my cat friend Rumpus enriched my life during all the years of my research and writing this book. My daily meditations in our beautiful garden and, in particular, my sacred grove have provided me with solace and insights into my work.

No photographer stands alone. I have benefited greatly by my long association with the Maine Photographic Workshops. I will always be grateful to Sam Abell, Kip Brundage, David Allan Harvey, Joe Baraban, Joyce Tennesen, Jay Maisel, and Chuck O'Rear. My images continue to improve because of the attitudes and techniques they taught. The photographs in this book were all taken with 35mm Nikon F3, 8008, F4, and F5 bodies using a variety of fixed focus and zoom lenses. Most of the film shot was Fuji Velvia and Provia, with some interior work done in Kodachrome 200. Interior lighting is either natural or provided by Nikon SB26 strobes. No photographs in this book have been taken without permission.

As this book has evolved, I have been in close contact with several museums who have expressed interest in exhibiting the photographs associated with it. I am particularly grateful to Stephen Markell of the Los Angeles County Museum of Art, Lisa Rebori of the Houston Museum of Natural Science, David Foster of the Field Museum of Chicago, Laurel Kendall and Rose Wadsworth of the American Museum of Natural History, and Aprile Gallant of the Portland Museum of Art in Maine.

I have long been an admirer of Thomas Moore, his thoughts and his writing. We became friends a few years ago, and I was very grateful when he offered to write the foreword to *Meeting God*. His response to the book and his articulate perception have been overwhelming. I am thrilled to be working again with Joseph Guglietti, who, with his assistant Lehze Flax, has sensitively transformed my photographs and writing into this beautiful volume. I am grateful to the integrity and foresight of Judith Joseph, my publishing consultant, who has helped me with every stage of the book's preparation, to the professionals at Yale University Press: Tina Weiner, Susan Donnelly, Mary Mayer, Rob Flynn, Alison Pratt, Heather D'Auria, and particularly my editors, Judy Metro and Heidi Downey, all of whom have worked diligently and insightfully to produce, promote, and market *Meeting God*, to Gail Rentsch and Jeany Wolf for their unflagging aid in the book's publicity, and to my superb personal assistant, Cheryl Smith, who has helped me to organize my thousands of slides into presentable form.

But, of course, this book really comes from my close relationship with India and her people: the innumerable friends I have in that subcontinent. I am so blessed. From my first moment there I have been accepted into the hearts and lives of countless Indians. I have lived in hundreds of Indian homes and had meals and tea in thousands of others. The people of India are remarkably generous with themselves, their possessions, their time, and their minds. Whatever I have learned is through the gifts of these friendships, of closely witnessing the rituals of home, family, and community, of learning from inside their meaning and value. I have been infused with the spirit of Hinduism.

Through Beatrice Wood I met and was sponsored in my work by two great Indian women: Kamaladevi Chattopadhyaya and Rukmini Devi Arundale. They kindly opened homes and doors for me everywhere. Two other great women also have been invaluable: Pupul Jayakar and Dr. Kapila Vatsyayan. For years I was closely associated with Kalakshetra College of Music and Dance in Madras, and I am particularly grateful to Shankara Menon, Kamala Trilokekar, Padmasini, K. Srinivasalu, and Peter and Sharada Hoffman. Others of particular importance in teaching me Hindu ethics and values have been Teni Sawhney, Mrs. Ram Lal, N. T. Vakani, P. P. Tewari, the family of Dulo Ram Sharma, Manvender and Siddhartha Singh, Mr. and Mrs. N. L. Tak, and their Highnesses the Maharajah and Maharani of Jodhpur, Gaj Singh and Hemlata Rajye. The single-minded faith of Bidulata Hota has exemplified Hindu devotion for me. Many non-Hindus have also helped me in my work, among them G. B., Dilgit, and Komal Singh, Mahaveer Swamy, Mahaveer Jain and Surendra Singh Chelawat and family. My close friends Prabhat and Sushmita Tandan and their daughters have discussed with me the fine points of this work. My research has been greatly aided by Dr. Jyotindra Jain, Dr. Anand Krishna, Dr. Kalyan Krishna, Dr. R. Nagaswami, Dr. M. S. Nagaraja Rao, Mahaveer Swami, Jyoti Bhatt, Amit Pasricha, P. R. Tippeswamy, Vidhu Shekhar Chaturvedi, and especially by Maheshwar Mohapatra.

Working closely with three sculptors of sacred votive terracottas, Vaithyalinga Pathar, Dibakar Muduli, and Ramdhari Prajapati, has given me insights into Hindu devotional reciprocity. My travel agents and friends at Gatik Ventures, Ltd., of New Delhi have gone way beyond the normal boundaries of their profession to facilitate my work, and three drivers (Anil "Papu" Sharma, Kalu Jena, and Andrew Shanthraj) have been of particular help to me.

Priests and temple authorities at hundreds of temples throughout India have welcomed me, answered my questions, and allowed me to photograph. I am particularly grateful to those in Tamil Nadu: the Meenakshi Sundareshwara Temple in Madurai, the Brihadeswara Temple in Thanjavur, the Ramalingeshwara Temple in Rameshwaram, the Virataneshwara Temple in Tiruvatigai, the Ranganatha Temple in Sri Rangam, Tiruchirapalli, the Sadhitapuramamman Temple in Samayapuram, the Punnalur Mariamman Temple in Punnalur, and the Nageshwara Temple in Kumbakonam, the Mundakanniamman Temple in Mylapore, Madras, and the many Ayyanar Koils throughout the state, particularly in South Arcot District; in Kerala: the Manarashala Temple in Haripad, the Valayal Devi Temple in Nadakkaval, the Chottanikkara Devi Temple near Cochin, and the Parabrahman Temple in Ochira; in Karnataka: the Chamundeshwari Temple in Mysore, the Kadri Manjunatha Temple in Dharmasthala, the Ganesha Temple in Indagunji, the Shri Krishna Temple in Udipi, the Marikhamba Temple in Sirsi, the Virupaksha Temple in Hampi, and the Kotilingeshwara Temple in Kamasandra; in Andhra Pradesh: the Venkateshwara Temple in Tirumala Temple and the Govindaraja Temple in Tirupati; in Orissa: the Santoshi Ma Temple in Bhubaneshwar, the Managala Thakurani Temple in Athagarh, the Batakapileshwara Temple in Nagpur, and the Gelubai Shrine in Padmapoda; in West Bengal: the Kalighat Temple in Calcutta, the Siddheswara Temple in Bhelulara, and the many Santhal shrines in the Sabarkone region of Bankura District; in Madhya Pradesh: the Mantangeshwara Temple in Khajuraho, the Thakurji Temple in Singhpur Charanpattika, and the many Bhilala shrines in Dhar and Alirajpur Districts; in Gujarat: the Swaminarayan Temples in Ahmedabad and Bhuj and the Jakh Temple in Kakadbhit; in Uttar Pradesh: the Vishvanatha, Annapurna, Durga and Asisangameshwara Temples in Varanasi, the many Kali-Ma Devasthanas in Deoria and Gorakhpur Districts, and the Mansa Devi Temple in Haridwar; in Rajasthan: the AmbaMataji and the BedlaMataji Temples in Udaipur, Eklingji Temple and the SriNathji Haveli in Nathdwara, the many Bhil shrines in Udaipur District, and the Laleshwar Mahadev Temple in Bikaner; in Himachal Pradesh: the Dhungri Temple in Manali, the Vaidyanath Temple in Baijnath, the Chamunda Temple in Nagarota and the Traari Cheleshwar Temple in Nagari. Aside from these, I have stopped at many hundreds of roadside shrines everywhere I have driven or walked throughout India. I have always been welcomed and have partaken in countless pujas. For these and so many other gestures of kindness, I am forever thankful.

One person has been pivotal to all my research for this book: Sunithi Narayan. She has traveled with me through many Indian states, opened countless doors to me, and her perception, wit, and wisdom are a constant source of knowledge from which much of my understanding comes.

Finally, I am grateful to the Hindu Gods and Goddesses themselves. In gathering my research and witnessing and photographing the pujas, I could not help but be affected by the deep spirituality resonant everywhere. Daily I have prayed to be an open channel for the messages of these deities and a bridge between East and West; and with my prayers has come a much deeper empathy for Hinduism. My prayers have grown to include acknowledgments of Ganesha, Surya, Lakshmi, Durga, Gelubai, Mariamman, Shiva, Shakti, Vishnu, Balaji, ShriNatji, and Parabrahman. I believe that without opening myself to these forces, the book would not have materialized in this form. I find it fascinating that through these prayers I have gained a deeper appreciation, understanding, and centering in my own religious heritage: the Christianity, beliefs, and sustaining faith of my family.

After a trip to India focused on Hindu rituals, a good friend, Linda Bailey, wrote the following poem, which sums up the transformative power of spirit:

*Celebrate this sacred space*
*Not because this space is sacred*
*Any space, in any place*
*Could be.*
*Celebrate because this place*
*Is where the veil hiding my face*
*Dropped*
*And let the healing grace*
*Invade my secret spaces.*

# INDEX

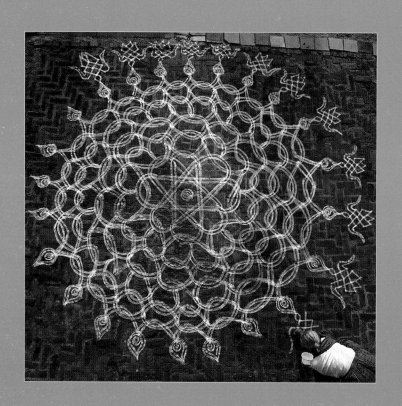